D0500420

the book of
hygge

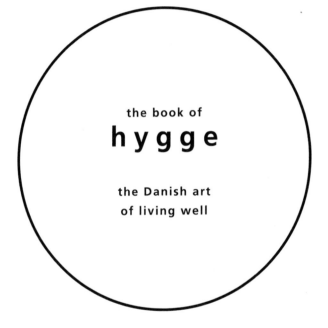

the book of

hygge

the Danish art
of living well

Louisa Thomsen Brits

Photography by Susan Bell

EBURY
PRESS

For my family

10 9 8 7 6 5 4 3

Ebury Press, an imprint of Ebury Publishing,
20 Vauxhall Bridge Road,
London SW1V 2SA

Ebury Press is part of the Penguin Random House
group of companies whose addresses can be found
at global.penguinrandomhouse.com

 Penguin
Random House
UK

Copyright © Louisa Thomsen Brits 2016
Photography © Susan Bell 2016

Louisa Thomsen Brits has asserted her right to be identified
as the author of this Work in accordance with the
Copyright, Designs and Patents Act 1988

First published by Ebury Press in 2016
www.penguin.co.uk

A CIP catalogue record for this book is available from the British Library

ISBN 9781785034466

Typeset by Seagull Design
Colour origination by Altaimage, London
Printed and bound in Italy by L.E.G.O. S.p.A

MIX
Paper from
responsible sources
FSC® C018179
www.fsc.org

Penguin Random House is committed to a sustainable
future for our business, our readers and our planet.
This book is made from Forest Stewardship Council®
certified paper.

Contents

Definition

Hygge (pronounced 'hue-gah') is a quality of presence and an experience of togetherness. It is a feeling of being warm, safe, comforted and sheltered.

Hygge is an experience of selfhood and communion with people and places that anchors and affirms us, gives us courage and consolation.

To hygge is to invite intimacy and connection. It's a feeling of engagement and relatedness, of belonging to the moment and to each other. Hygge is a sense of abundance and contentment. Hygge is about being not having.

Note from the author

Hygge is a feeling that most of us know but can't quite define. To give a name to an experience is to pay attention to it. Hygge can describe feelings that are already familiar to you. It is there in the rhythm of your daily life, in your habits, routines and rituals.

You don't need Danish recipes or the secrets of a Scandinavian lifestyle to learn how to hygge. It can be found in asking yourself where you feel most at home, what are the activities and customs that anchor you, who makes you feel at ease, what is it that contributes most to your sense of wellbeing, what do you do to unwind, what do you reach for to create comfort?

For me, hygge exists in moments of contentment, particularly at the beginning and end of the day. We hygger first thing in the morning when we light a candle at our breakfast table, make coffee, pancakes and packed lunches and when we return home to each other to share a cup of tea or a glass of wine, to sit around the kitchen table together and enjoy our evening meal.

I invite hygge by lighting fires almost every day, inside or out, by spending time with the people I love and enjoying time alone. Hygge is held in the ritual of the bedtime stories that I have read for the past twenty-three years, in birthday celebrations and the enchantment of Christmas Eve. To celebrate the seasons, I swim in the river all year round, walk the dogs in the fields at night and bathe outside. I hygger when I make risotto, make love, make tea or read in bed. I find it at the heart of the dance floor, when I walk through our local town, camp at small festivals or meet a friend for coffee. It lives in my father's study, in my mother's garden, around the table in my aunts' quiet apartments in Århus, on the veranda under a wide African sky with my husband's family. Hygge arrives when all four children come home and we sit by a fire under the oak trees in the garden, play cards, beachcomb, dance in the kitchen or curl up under blankets to watch a film together.

I hope that I can translate hygge from a very Danish word to the universal language that it is and that, in reading this book, you will discover the hygge that already exists in your life and become attuned to its presence.

Introduction

It's marvellous to be – one should never be anything else.

Mogens Lorentzen

The word hygge has been sifted to the surface in recent years but the concept is not new. It is a practice as old as sitting around a fire or sharing food with a friend. Words emerge from culture, history, topography and place. They're formed by time and habit and are passed from one generation to the next through stories, ritual and values. Hygge helps us to communicate what it's like to be human; it is part of a global vocabulary that speaks to our humanity and addresses our basic human need to belong. It's an old word for a new language that we are beginning to explore in order to share values common to us all.

Happiness is like a butterfly;
the more you chase it, the more
it will elude you, but if you turn
your attention to other things,
it will come and sit softly on
your shoulder.

Henry David Thoreau

The Danes, considered to be among the happiest
people in the world, have enjoyed hygge for hundreds
of years. Denmark's high standard of living, decent
health care, gender equality, accessible education and
equitable distribution of wealth all contribute to the
measurable happiness of the Danish people. But a
determined pursuit of happiness doesn't necessarily lead
to wellbeing. At the heart of Danish life, and at the core
of hygge, is the deeper stability of contentment.

When we are content, our daily actions are infused
with a quiet satisfaction that we share with those
around us. We become aware of and responsible for
other people's wellbeing and they, in turn, for ours.
Hygge captures a way of being with other people,
caring for them and ourselves.

In our overstretched, complex lives, hygge is an uncomplicated daily practice that engages us, keeping us attuned to our surroundings and open to empathy and wonder.

Hygge is part of the language of human action and interaction all over the world. To hygge is a universal impetus revealed in the small rituals, gestures and daily experiences that unite and define us all.

We all hygger: gathered around a table for a shared meal or beside a fire on a dark night, when we sit in the corner of our local café or wrap ourselves in a blanket at the end of a day on the beach. Lying spoons, baking in a warm kitchen, bathing by candlelight, being alone in bed with a hot water bottle and a good book – these are all ways to hygge. Hygge draws meaning from the fabric of ordinary living. It's a way of acknowledging the sacred in the secular, of giving something ordinary a special context, spirit and warmth and taking time to make it extraordinary.

Many of men pursue pleasure with such breathless haste that they hurry past it.

Søren Kierkegaard

Hygge happens when we commit to the pleasure of the present moment in its simplicity. It's there in the things we do that give everyday life value and meaning, that comfort us, make us feel at home, rooted and generous.

At a time of global instability we have become distanced from each other and the environment. We have lost the immediacy, comfort and truthfulness of the literal and actual, and need to find alternative ways to consume and connect. Hygge describes a way of being that introduces humanity and warmth into our homes, schools, workplaces, cities and nations.

Hygge stems from a society that is focused on people rather than things. It is linked to the language of love and to the idea that real wealth is not what we can accumulate but what we have to share.

History

Hygge has been a practice and an icon of the Danish nation for many years. It is one of the everyday words that tells the story of the backdrop to Danish life. The word stems from the Old Norse word *hu* – meaning thought, mind, courage. The Old Norse form *hyggja* (aligned with Old English *hycgan* and Old High

German *hyggen*) means to think. Hygge was borrowed from the Norwegians in the late nineteenth or early twentieth century; in Middle Danish the word hygge means to console or encourage.

What is Danish in Denmark is so obvious to the foreigner there. *Hygge* (cosiness), *tryghed* (security) and *trivsel* (wellbeing) are the three graces of Danish culture and socialization.

Jonathan M. Schwartz

Danes are good at appreciating the small things in life and at making the best of whatever they have. They place emphasis on the inner sphere of people, places and things. Modern Denmark emerged from the gradual dissolution of the large historical Danish Empire that once stretched from Greenland to Iceland, over Norway, Southern Sweden, Northern Germany and present-day Denmark to the Islands of the Baltic. But after being forced to cede a large portion of its territory, including the dramatic, mountainous landscape of Norway in the nineteenth century, the Danes began to identify with smallness and with interior landscape. The military failure of the old empire was subsequently not mourned as an outward loss but celebrated as an inward gain. Danes didn't just make do with the gentler forms of lowlands and many small islands – they came to idealize them. They looked inside for identity and placed significance on inner space as a reality in its own right.

The new Denmark's national identity was shaped by the enlightenment and particularly by the teachings of Nikolaj Frederik Severin Grundtvig (born 1783–1872) and his project of *folkeoplysning* – inclusive, popular enlightenment. He embraced the enlightenment values associated with personal freedom, was inspired by ancient Norse mythology and was, above all else, anti-elitist. Grundtvig believed that national identity was about a sense of belonging, that Denmark should not pursue outer grandeur but seek prosperity in the wellbeing of its people, and that education and good living should be made available to all Danes, particularly the peasant farmer masses who made up most of society. He became the leader of the Danish Folk High School

movement that offered learning for life. He taught mainly through songs and hymns, establishing a tradition of community singing that continues to this day. Most Danish households still have a copy of the Folk High School Songbook. On many occasions throughout the year, Danes still sing the ideologically packed songs that affirm the ideas of simplicity, cheerfulness, reciprocity, community and belonging that are cornerstones of hygge.

Hygge is a product of the very particular social ethos that developed in Denmark in the late nineteenth and early twentieth century. During that time there was a shift in focus in urban industrial society towards leisure, authenticity, scientific rationality and the comforts of home and domestic life. Elite culture was deplored as shallow by the growing middle classes who placed emphasis on family and intimacy.

Denmark's history, its egalitarianism, liberalism and emphasis on individual freedom and wellbeing have granted the Danes an ability to participate in the moment. Hygge facilitates that to happen. It is a word that unlocks a small universe of meaning and possibility for all of us to enjoy.

In this book

Being Danish isn't a prerequisite to understanding and enjoying hygge. We all recognize the universal themes that underpin the practice – belonging, trust, connection, community, mutuality, kinship, security, home, contentment, authenticity, presence and love.

This book is an invitation to make small shifts of practice and perception in order to invite more hygge into everyday life. It is an exploration of the concept and a practical guide.

Hygge gives us a framework to support our very human needs, desires and habits. There is a simple, material structure beneath the immaterial rewards. To learn to hygge is to take practical steps to evoke it – to shelter, cluster, enclose, embrace, comfort and warm ourselves and each other. Cultivating the habits of balance, moderation, care and observance will then comfortably ensure more hygge in our daily lives.

For such an uncomplicated experience, hygge is a many-layered concept, a total phenomenon that loses some of its meaning when separated into individual elements. Each of the following chapters includes both immaterial and material aspects of hygge, because they are inextricably linked. Although the

way that we hygger is unique to each of us, throughout the book there are suggestions of how to weave hygge into daily life.

Underlying themes

There are three salient themes that run through any experience of hygge – interiority, contrast and atmosphere. They support and extend each other and shape our understanding of the concept.

Interiority

Within hygge is an awareness of both inner and outer space. Interiority is a perception of being a discrete, bounded presence that exists in relation to others, to place and to the passage of time. When we hygger, we feel located and sheltered but aware that our shelter has boundaries, physical and temporal. Hygge comes from a culture that values the notion of inner space and celebrates a quiet stability of individual identity. Mind, home and country are the interiorities of hygge.

It makes sense that the everyday experience and practice of something like hygge would not be reserved only for Scandinavians, but shared with other societies that nurture the idea of interiority to the extent that they foreground it.

Jeppe Trolle Linnet

Contrast

Because interiority focuses on the inside-outside aspect of hygge, it introduces the important theme of contrast. When we hygger there is a sense of distance between us and the outside world, a contrast between the feeling that we are at the still axis of a moment of pleasure and our awareness of ever-moving life around us.

Our experience of contrast is heightened by spatial, temporal and social conditions – inside versus outside, shelter versus exposure, warm versus cold, day versus night, light versus shadow, stillness versus activity, indulgence versus restraint, relaxation versus work, independence versus society, equality versus hierarchy, peace versus conflict.

Atmosphere

Hygge is often supplemented by the Danish notion of *stemning* or atmosphere. To hygge is to create a harmonious atmosphere, a feeling of warmth, a mood of contentment.

Usage

Hygge is freely used to describe rooms, buildings, homes, parties, people and activities.

Hygge is frequently used in everyday language in these forms:

Noun

Hygge

Verbs

Infinitive – basic form of the verb – at hygge
There are two hygge-related verbs:

1.

Hygger – present indicative verbal form, a new
    non-reflexive verb
Hyggede (past verbal form)

At have det hyggeligt – 'to have it hyggelig': to be in
   a situation characterized by hygge

2.
Hygger sig – an older form; the light reflexive verb
   (to hygge oneself/themselves)
Hygger sig describes the experience of hygge alone
   with an emphasis on personal feelings of wellbeing.

The light reflexive particle *sig* encodes personal
perspective but cancels some of the social
connotations of hygge.

Phrases using the verb hygge are commonly used in
everyday speech, particularly when saying goodbye:

   Hyg dig!
   Ka' du hygge dig!
   Du må hygge dig!

They mean 'Have hygge!' – similar to 'Have fun!' in
English, but with rich meaning attached.

Adjective
Hyggelig (hygge-like)
Det var hyggeligt – that was hyggeligt

An adjective that describes an event or moment:
e.g. en hyggelig aften – 'a hyggelig evening'

Or a place, e.g. en hyggelig by – 'a hyggelig town/a town with hygge'

Compound words are often used

Nouns:

Hyggeaften – a hygge evening

Hyggebelysning – hyggelighting

Hjemmehygge – home hygge

Hyggekrog – hygge corner

Råhygge – strong, authentic hygge

Julehygge – Christmas hygge

Verbs:

At julehygge – to Christmas hygge

At hyggesnakke – to hygge-chat

1: Belonging

The greatest hazard of all, losing one's self, can occur very quietly in the world, as if it were nothing at all. No other loss can occur so quietly; any other loss – an arm, a leg, five dollars, a wife, etc. – is sure to be noticed.

Søren Kierkegaard

Togetherness

At the heart of hygge is an experience of belonging and a sense of connection. It's most often associated with being in the company of others, but we can enjoy hygge alone.

Hygge satisfies our natural longing to belong. Like the emergence of fireflies, when we hygger we shine individually but glow in unison to reveal an inclination towards a powerful collective harmony. It is a practice that connects our individual experience, our feelings of mutuality with others, our collective ideals and the tangible qualities of objects, spaces and places.

Hygge can be found in the settings where we feel most comfortably human, that give us context, offer identity, relation and history. We hygger on our porch swings, armchairs, doorsteps and in our beds, local bars, village halls and bookshops.

To be in a situation characterized by hygge is to be in a state of pleasant wellbeing and security, with a relaxed frame of mind and an open enjoyment of the immediate situation in all its small pleasures – a state one achieves most often with close members of one's social network in a home-like setting.

Judith Friedman Hansen

The importance of place

When we hygger, we feel firmly emplaced – anchored and present. We thrive on a strong sense of place. Our souls are fed by the predictable rhythm of returning to settings that are comforting in their familiarity – a local coffee shop, a particular tree, an aunt's quiet apartment, a regular swimming spot.

Hygge is a phenomenon that reflects our way of inhabiting the world. The routines that shape our days locate us – from the places we visit to the small rituals that give us pause. Drinking tea first thing in the morning from a favourite mug and stopping for a glass of wine on a friend's porch on the way home from work confirm our feelings of rootedness and make us feel an integral part of our environment.

Human connection is the glue that binds us in an experience of hygge. Life in Denmark is harnessed to community, and Danes grow up with a strong sense of connection to their home, their street, their country.

When we hygger, we unwrap a package of good feelings to share with each other and offer signs of encouragement and symbols of inclusion; we make arrangements that provide warmth, shelter, nourishment and comfort – by doing something as simple as lighting a candle at dinner, pulling up chairs

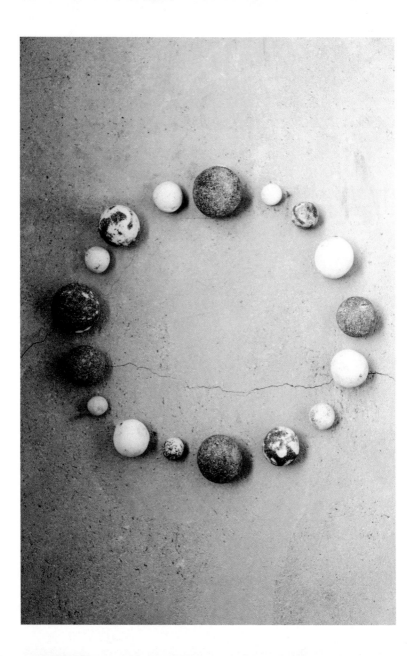

and sitting together for a shared meal, or taking cake into the office and inviting others stop for long enough to enjoy a slice with a cup of coffee.

Wherever we gather in the spirit of hygge, whether it's beside a barbecue on a beach or around a table in a bar on a cold autumn night, we feel anchored in one place.

Circle of warmth

To hygge is to create an enclosing circle of warmth. The primal comfort of an open fire and good company on a dark night are the epitome of hygge. A cluster of people sitting beneath the encircling glow of a pendant lamp hung low over a table is a common sight in Denmark – the light seems to hold everyone together, to define them as a unit.

Clustering together

Hygge is a physical and psychological clustering together for affirmation and a sense of belonging.

In Denmark, most gatherings are patterned by a cluster of people sharing a single focus of awareness that everyone helps to sustain – commonly a table surrounded by people pressed together and united in maintaining conversation, like keeping a fire burning in the hearth.

Danes prefer to gather in limited numbers rather than in large, expansive groups, to emphasize the unity of their small circles. Bubbles of interaction are everywhere – outside on a street lined with cafés, and in the privacy of their homes. Everyone creates their own groups, their own foundations for hygge. Although it's a pattern of behaviour that the Danes have carefully honed, but it's a non-verbal vocabulary that belongs to us all. Hygge happens wherever people gather in a wholehearted and inclusive way, whether it's an unexpected encounter on a pavement or for a birthday celebration in a kitchen. Hygge is about human connection.

There are times when we find ourselves in the role of a stranger standing on the margins, examining everything that seems to be unquestionable to members of an inner circle. The centripetal force of mutuality, warmth and enthusiasm that binds a group is sometimes intimidating and impenetrable. Feeling excluded from a group is uncomfortable. Feeling trapped inside one is equally disquieting. There is the downside that the Danish style of socializing could be considered exclusive.

But hygge is a process that usually draws a person in and invites engagement. In the face of tensions that threaten to pull families, friends and colleagues apart, an experience of hygge helps bind us together.

Family

Hygge can often be distilled to an experience of kinship, of being with those who understand you and signal that you are wholly accepted.

True kinship takes a warm heart. In essence, it is about being together, deeply honestly. We talk about love so much but we forget that it is something we give rather than get: a way of being.

Ilse Crawford

There is an honesty to a hyggelig encounter that echoes the dynamics of ideal family life. Hygge and our ideas of family are interwoven, both associated with care and intimacy. Many of us think of family as a place that satisfies the heart. Addressing the needs of the heart, warmth, amity and belonging are the essence of what we experience and offer when we hygger. We feel warmed when we step into a hyggeligt environment. We can be unguarded, carefree and willing to be seen.

If we're fortunate, we can be our most unselfconscious with our relations and those who share the places we inhabit – our homes and our communities. The word inhabit comes from a root that means to give and to receive, and hygge stems from reciprocity and love.

Considering family togetherness seems promising for understanding hygge in its most basic form. When we refer to hygge, we are using the concept of home and family to think with.

Jeppe Trolle Linnet

Family is cherished in Scandinavian culture, and even though it is far from reality in many places, the ideal of a stable family remains a touchstone for many Danes. Regardless of its shape, modern family is seen as a place of intimacy and integration that can prepare and restore each family member for encounters with the outside world.

Work

Danes are innately sceptical about the value of strategic manoeuvring at home or at work. They have a desire to be seen in the fullness of who they are, wherever they are. In Denmark, professional environments often display the qualities that many of us would associate with a familial context – informality, casual dress and comfortable furniture arranged to encourage familiarity and diminish isolation. Danish working culture is based on open communication, collaboration and flat hierarchy. Employees are considered team members.
Each person is expected to take their personal responsibilities seriously in return for influence and the degree of flexibility required to have a career without compromising work-life balance.

Knowing that our individual contribution is recognized and working together as a team give us a sense of belonging. Work can be an experience of hygge for as long as it's possible to maintain an even and comfortable pace. If we become too busy, our time cramped with many activities, hygge disappears.

Trust

There's a freedom of self-expression implicit in hygge that rests on reciprocity and mutual trust. Embedded in an experience of hygge is a shared belief that good things will happen, and that all members of a group will be given equal voice and offered recognition. Everyone present is considered part of a greater whole. Each person wants everyone else to feel good.

Understanding that we are welcome encourages us to let go and allow ourselves to be seen without the need to perform or scramble for attention.

Hygge invites feelings of harmony and mutuality that overcome barriers and facilitate communication; we no longer feel separate when we hygger. The shape of family life has changed; many of us live alone. We look for belonging and connection in our local

communities – in cafés, corner shops and restaurants. We can hygge to help bridge the space between being alone and feeling lonely.

Participants experience a 'social intimacy' and a basic 'trust' in the inclusiveness and good intentions of the other people present. Hygge cannot be achieved if there is disagreement and conflict in the group or if there is a sense of mistrust between people. Furthermore, situations characterized by hygge eschew graveness and seriousness.

Carsten Levisen

We usually hygger to establish a human factor in our lives, to enjoy the warm aura of friendship and the security of kinship, the benefits of shared activity, physical closeness and the warmth of proximity.

A rich social life (measured by quality of experience rather than quantity of friends) contributes to good health, happiness and longevity. So many of us place value on hard work, measurable achievement and wealth, and often fail to set aside time to nurture our relationships and strengthen social ties. We make the mistake of believing that security is found in material things rather than people.

In quieting our ambition on occasion to concentrate on empathy and friendship, we are still investing in ourselves and we diminish the likelihood of minor aliments, increase our lifespan and improve our capacity to fight disease.

In paying attention to our wellbeing, we address the needs of our environment – the society that we live in and our planet. Sustainability depends on community – when we learn to be happily reliant on each other, we're less likely to turn to material consumption to meet our emotional needs.

Belonging to the moment

Hygge helps us to enter a moment or a place. By appealing to our senses and promising security, it draws us in, atuning us to the spirit of a location, inviting us to relax and connect to ourselves and to others. It facilitates a sense of being fully present and opens us to the pleasures of the occasion.

There is a slight anxiety implicit in hygge that heightens our experience of belonging to the moment – the knowledge that there is a world of activity and responsibility just beyond the instant, poised to impose, intertwines with our situation, enlivening us to its particulars and pleasures. The flip side of an experience of enjoyment is the certainty that it won't last forever. Today's moment of hygge will be tomorrow's memory. With that awareness, we give ourselves over to the moment more completely.

It must be emphasized that hygge entails commitment to the present moment and a readiness to set distractions aside.

Judith Friedman Hansen

Hygge is evoked in situations where there is nothing to accomplish but letting go to the present moment in a way that's more aligned to simple pleasure than deep reflection.

Experiencing a sense of presence and belonging is challenging when we're stressed or distracted. Hygge isn't the complete absence of the usual demands of a fully engaged human life, but it is facilitated by a willingness to put down our problems and abandon our cares for a while.

At the heart of hygge is a willingness to set aside time for simply being with people and, ideally, having all the time in the world for them. Hygge is a vehicle for showing that we care. It's a way of paying attention to our children or partners and friends in the messy reality of the here and now, and putting down the distractions that pull us in different directions. So many of us are drawn to a virtual world of connectivity. Hygge isn't about a life without technology, but it asks us to balance our commitments and remember the value of human interaction, conversation and physical intimacy. It liberates us to fully inhabit the moment without feeling compelled to record it.

Spontaneity and immediacy characterize hygge, as does a willingness to accept our differences and enjoy an atmosphere of tolerance and peace.

...the salient feature of hygge
is the atmosphere of warm and
relaxed enjoyment of the moment
which it allows. While it is nurtured
by thoughtfulness and mutual
involvement, hygge is informal
and unrestrained.

Judith Friedman Hansen

When we feel held by the atmosphere of a place or captured by the pleasure of an encounter, hygge is being evoked. Atmosphere binds us together, weaves us into the particulars of a place and makes us feel at home with ourselves and with those around us.

Belonging to ourselves

Achieving the serenity and freedom of feeling that we belong to ourselves, wherever we are, is a common concern in our mobile lives. The practice of hygge can instill stability of presence, a state of awareness and ease by creating a frame around us, offering us comfort, giving us a point of focus and allowing us to relax enough to be ourselves.

Hygge relies on us finding a balance between self-containment and wholehearted participation, personal liberty and awareness of the needs of others. It connotes a caring, civilised mode of behaviour that builds companionable ease and trust.

The most common form of despair is not being who you are.
Søren Kierkegaard

In Denmark, the ability to be at peace with oneself is a character trait that is highly respected. A person who simply lives up to their own standards and appears at ease in their environment, who seems to eschew jostling for a place in social hierarchy and competitive behaviour is described as able to *hvile i sig selv* – rest in oneself, be comfortable in one's own skin. It is a quality that suggests an inner stability of identity that is not dependent on attention or status. Holding on to our identity is a challenge for all of us. Often it is easier on home ground where we operate in a knowable sphere. And easier in a country like Denmark where there are not huge disparities between people, so their identities are less likely to be usurped by their social or professional position.

Fostering togetherness

People who are innately comfortable hygger with ease. They are less self-conscious or over-involved in their own self-presentation, and unlikely to indulge in one-upmanship. Those who are prepared to leave their problems at the door, who aren't preoccupied with the concerns of their lives outside of the hyggelig sphere, also support the dynamics of hygge.

...to create a sense of belonging takes dedicated time and space to listen and to care for each other, whether we are talking about the extended family, a nuclear family, a couple or friends.

Isle Crawford

Being too preoccupied with how a gathering is taking shape, and making obvious attempts to take personal responsibility for the smooth running of an event, will diminish the flame at the heart of hygge.

The Danish concern for harmony and amicability is reflected in a pervading emphasis on the embracing integrity of the social milieu. On many levels, in many different contexts, Danes seek to include all individuals present in an overriding sense of relatedness.

Judith Friedman Hansen

When Danes get together the principle of inclusion manifests. No one is wilfully excluded from conversation. Balance between individuals is casually but carefully maintained and hostility, aggression and overt competition are suppressed. Everyone is amicably concerned with maintaining the comfortable nature

45

of the gathering and staying focused on mutual enjoyment. They consistently make an effort to include others in an experience of collective harmony and to ensure that everyone feels a sense of belonging and relatedness. This comes with an abiding sense of responsibility towards others, and informs the shape of Danish life from social gatherings to the welfare system.

Hygge relates to social awareness, ways of communicating and ways of thinking about others. When we hygger, we acknowledge each other's traits and foibles without indulging them.

Competitiveness threatens balance and jeopardizes the abiding sense of everyone being a part of one cohesive experience. The Danish expression *gå i selvsving,* 'go into self-oscillation', describes people who have stopped listening to others and endlessly repeat their own ideas, immune to signs of disapproval and apparently uninterested in congruity of the group.

To hold on to hygge, we learn to listen and to speak up. We hone the art of conversation and attempt to master an evenness of flow (an equal share of contributions and turns), and to maintain a sense of mutual involvement. Those of us who are more introverted can relax in the knowledge that no one is expected to take centre stage. For an occasion to work well for everyone, the desire for hygge has to be balanced with a respect for individuality.

Hygge is 'fragile' because the process, in a sense, *is* the goal. It comes through collaborative effort and can easily appear but also easily disappear.

Carsten Levisen

In Denmark, conversing without conflict is called *samtale* or 'together talk'. The content of this light conversation is less important than the interaction it facilitates. There is consensus, if not complicity. Danes are reluctant to grant superiority to others, so topics of conversation that depend on reference to authority are adeptly sidestepped.

Hyggelige conversations are not meant to be debate. They don't need preparation or require that we bolster ourselves with facts and knowledge. We can relax and collectively foster new ideas. If we are too serious, the spirit of hygge will evaporate. It's a

state of social nirvana in Denmark – a way of simply feeling really good, right now. No one believes it will last forever.

Egalitarian society

Hygge comes from a society that prioritizes tender values and is shaped by the patterns of egalitarian behaviour. It doesn't permit any participant to dominate a gathering or take centre stage for long. Danes have a strong cultural aversion towards aggressive behaviour and cooperate to avoid contentious issues or divisive topics. Despite a firm belief in the rights of an individual, most Danes live in a world of quiet conformity, paying exceptionally high taxes and individually accepting a high degree of social and environmental accountability. Danes do not view their investment as an easy route to divesting themselves of responsibility to the state – they consider their individual contribution a benefit to the common good. The dynamics of hygge echo those sentiments.

The Danes are not a nation...
they are a tribe, this is the
strength of their fellowship and
the reason that they have
unshakeable trust in each other.

Knud Jespersen

Hygge is a place of safety, warmth and welcome that can exist because there are rules of engagement in place. Each participant tacitly agrees to behave in a considerate and mutually supportive way. Everyone holds on to the fabric of hygge, woven collectively by the way that they conduct themselves.

Samfund – the Danish word for society as a whole – has a connotation of community. It's not an unexamined idyll. No public institution is granted immunity from popular criticism. Few individuals can breach accepted codes of behaviour without light but levelling sanctions. Anyone displaying an inflated sense of their own worth, or who is thought to be taking themselves too seriously, is likely to be teased or subjected to barbed jokes. If they respond with good humour, they are swiftly forgiven so that everyone can continue to sail happily downstream together.

A Dane will tend to consider any other person as neither better nor lesser than himself, while acknowledging, for example, that the other person may incidentally have more money or a lower status.

Judith Friedman Hansen

Within most Danes is a kernel of internalized sanction that keeps their behaviour from sliding into self-indulgence or pomposity and disrupting the balance of a hyggelig gathering. There are diverse and subtle ways in which social order is maintained – the Danes are connoisseurs of guilt and commonly use it combined with gentle humour as a non-aggressive deterrent to uphold the quality of human relationships.

As a marker for authentic and acceptable behaviour, hygge can be a vehicle for social control. The rhetoric of hygge can be used as a way to ensure that individuals remain within a narrow band of social mobility.

Jante law

In a fictional account of a small Danish town, the Danish-Norwegian author Aksel Sandemose drew up a set of ten rules, *janteloven*, the jante law, that defined the social control and forces of envy that shadow egalitarian society, sanctioning the behaviour of anyone aspiring to a bigger, better life.

In considering these fictional rules, Danes unite in opposition, or ask themselves how they should behave and treat each other, to both protect the privilege of individualism and create a society where everyone can thrive.

National pride is strong in Denmark. Danes could be considered ethnocentric if their nationalism is seen to be attached to the kind of behaviour that displays a fear of those who are different from themselves. Danes want to maintain their comfortable equilibrium but they are a conscious and caring nation. It is a struggle for many Danes to show welcome to all and, at the same time, meet a natural need to protect their own cultural boundaries. Perhaps the language of hygge can translate across cultural divides between us all. The values that support hygge and underpin egalitarian society suggest the possibility of a way of being where every living thing is recognized for its unique qualities and upheld as part of an integrated whole.

2: Shelter

Hygge is housed by an experience of shelter, and the foundation of our shelter is our basic sense of security. In Denmark, the notion of security, or *tryghed*, is part of the supporting framework of daily life. It's an experience of everyday wellbeing, safety, peace of mind and freedom rolled together. Trust, familiarity and predictability give it dimension and stability. Danish life is reliably unsurprising and safe, and the starting point of an encounter between two Danes is trust, affording the Danish people the opportunity to meet each other with openness and respect, and creating the basic structure of hygge.

Danes enjoy the shelter of kinship and make time for the comfort and retreat of hygge. The landscape of everyday life is dotted with temporary shelters from the pressures of work and responsibility, moments of relatedness built into each day – as simple as a quiet bath, a midweek dinner with friends or a weekend morning in bed for the whole family with a full coffee pot and a pile of newspapers and magazines. Hygge affords us places to catch our breath and feel the richness of life. But they are islands of respite rather than refuge, pause not escape.

Like children enjoying a camp beneath a blanket stretched between two chairs, we all need to build shelter from time to time. The pleasure and intimacy of sheltering is charged by the sounds of life revolving around us. Whether we are under an umbrella on a pavement wrapped in complicity and conversation, or alone immersed in the pages of a good book, we're happily held in our private sphere but still conscious of the shape of our sanctuary.

Sheltering each other

To hygge is to build sanctuary. The most basic security that we can provide each other is shelter – physical and psychological. We shelter each other when we invite people into our homes, when we give time, listen well or provide a bed for the night; when we offer privacy, a winged armchair, anonymity, a tent in the garden, a night in a hostel.

It is in the shelter of each other that the people live.

Irish proverb

Showing neighbourly consideration shelters others from our noise. In quietly paying someone else's bill, we shelter them from external pressures or discomfort. Reading to a child envelops them in another world. Shutting down our computers or drawing the curtains prevents the rest of the world from intruding for a while. We find a haven in the community of a quiet church or a noisy café. Wherever we seek shelter, hygge can bind us together, levelling status differences and providing momentary sanctuary from the demands of daily life, from loneliness, disharmony, social climbing and competition.

I felt it shelter to speak to you.

Emily Dickinson

From the outside, a sheltered life looks inviting, but there are shadows on the periphery of the warmth, safety and comfort – the greyness of boredom, a longing for a more exotic life, a hint of exclusivity and a fear of the strange and unfamiliar. However, even from the protected sphere of our own homes we can live expansive and generous lives. Technology is widening our horizons and helping us to explore our natural propensity to trust, share and exchange, transcending nationality and economic status, removing traditional boundaries and social barriers. We have new opportunities to overcome our differences and to find shelter in our commonality and humanity.

Kinship is thriving on mutual sheltering. There is a global community creating an alternative socio-economic system with communication, sharing and collaboration at its heart. This encourages us to profit from our interconnectedness by sharing ideas, exchanging goods and offering each other affordable sanctuary across the world, by accepting strangers to stay in our homes. This phenomenon of global citizenship is a manifestation of the values that underpin hygge.

Building shelter

The word hygge houses a small universe of meaning.
When we hygger we build a place of prospect and
refuge, a framework that makes us feel enclosed
and reassured. The architecture of the shelter that
we create is physical and psychological. It is made up
of the places where we find sanctuary, the bonds of
our relationships, our habits and daily rituals, and is
furnished with the things that mean most to us.

I see the task of architecture as the defence of the authenticity of human experience.

Juhani Pallasmaa

We need places that respond to our unique rhythms,
to the movements of our bodies; places that cradle
and embrace us. Ideally buildings and cities would be
designed with our enduring human needs in mind.

Embrace

When we reach a place of shelter, we feel held. Like the material and moral structure of a home that supports and protects our bodies, and centres us in the world, a truly hyggelig place or encounter echoes the sheltering of a nest. It is both open and embracing, allowing us to relax and to dwell for long enough to feel restored.

When we hygger, we nest into the setting offered to us. Our feelings are held in our bodies, our bodies are nested into the location and the location is nested successively into a building, garden, street, city, landscape, the wider world. In the embrace of a hyggeligt environment, whether it's a downtown bar or neighbour's kitchen, we feel that we can relax, curl up and rest.

To curl up belongs to the phenomenology of the verb to inhabit, and only those who have learned to do so can inhabit with intensity.

Gaston Bachelard

Hygge is the perfect response to the patterns of human behaviour – it accommodates the movement that springs from our desire to explore and achieve and supports our need to be momentarily held, wherever we are.

Hygge is a release and an exchange; a fusion of our sense of self, the place we occupy and the people around us. Because hygge relaxes us, it affords us the possibility of fully inhabiting a place and a moment. The word 'inhabit' comes from the Latin *habere* which meant 'to hold' in offering or receiving. We don't need the same surroundings to hygge, but we do need to feel held.

Enclosure

The theme of an enclosed, secure space is intrinsic to hygge. Protective boundaries lend the possibility of savouring the present moment undisturbed, affording us peace of mind. To feel safe, we need to be able to read the secrets of a place, to know the texture of its shadows and the shape of the perimeter. With a clear line of sight and the assurance of being uninterrupted, almost anywhere can be a refuge.

A circle of lamplight carves a shelter in surrounding darkness. An evening spent deep in conversation with

63

friends with no external obligations pulling us apart contains both a sense of mutual involvement and an awareness of the stream of life flowing around us. Our interaction feels contained by an invisible shield between our gathering and the rest of the world.

Life begins well. It begins enclosed, protected, all warm in the bosom of the house.

Gaston Bachelard

An essential ingredient to hygge is the boundary that marks a place or delineates a moment – a fence, a circle of cushions or a stolen half hour. The boundaries that we put in place when we hygger can be both physical and temporal – setting aside an hour to visit a friend, pulling chairs into a circle around a campfire or closing the door to secure a den to watch a film in peace. When we arrange office furniture, decide where to sit on a bus or set out a picnic rug, we establish a boundary and a point of focus and make space for the spirit of hygge to breathe life and warmth into our activities.

When we establish limits, we can relax and dwell in a place or moment. Our dreams, thoughts and conversations can unfurl in peace. We find ourselves in a place where we can believe that good things will happen.

Our beds are a haven when life is challenging. A bed pushed into a corner, with walls on two sides, or an hour spent curled up under a blanket, recall the primal pleasure of a *hule*, or cave. Box beds with wooden panelling on all sides were traditional in Scandinavia as far back as the Iron Age. *Himmelseng* (heaven beds) hung with canopies and filled with thick quilts were where people kept each other warm through long winter nights. Shutters, wooden doors, low ceilings and thick curtains all help us to feel secure.

To shield themselves from others or, conversely, from the chill of loneliness and an uninhabited room, a Dane might make *hyggekrog* or *hygge hjorne* (hygge corners) by screening a corner, delineating a space with wood or fabric, or creating a window seat to furnish with comfort. A mezzanine elevates us to a place of prospect and privacy. Pulling furniture together articulates the hope of connection and helps us create shelter in our (often temporary) homes.

Contrast

A sense of contrast highlights the security we feel when we hygger. We are happily set apart but conscious of everything that surrounds us. Hygge relies on an interplay between presence and absence – the unheard dialogue between everything tangible and concrete around us and all that we cannot see on the periphery of the moment.

Enjoying the stillness of early morning before a day gathers its usual pace is an awareness of both contrast and temporary shelter that serves to give us perspective.

Sheltering from the rain in a warm car or sitting on a window seat as night falls, with nothing to attend to but the twilight, is a kind of shelter. Looking up at our own line of illuminated windows from a darkening street heightens our appreciation when we finally step into our home at the end of the day.

Human scale

A hyggelig building is human in scale. It's built in reasonable proportion to the people who live or work there to create an environment that is relatable and easy to grasp. Large, open places are rarely seen as hyggelige. Spaces that are of manageable proportion, that feel relaxed and down to earth, most easily effect the emergence of hygge.

The structure of life I have described in buildings – the structure which I believe to be objective – is deeply and inextricably connected with the human person, and with the innermost nature of human feeling.

Christopher Alexander

Towns and cities in Denmark often have low-rise buildings, the embrace of town squares, courtyards and streets just wide enough to cross with ease. Many Danish homes are built to respond to the ebb and flow of domestic life and to the changing seasons. They invite the light but celebrate the dark, with fireplaces and areas built to enfold and comfort. With a robust but sensual practicality, intimacy and openness are

held in balance. Spaces are created for solitude and participation, privacy and sociability, stillness and sound. Nature is encouraged to embrace a home, to grow close to its walls, to shade and intertwine with the lives of the people who live there.

The majority of us live in buildings that haven't been built with us in mind. We spend our lives in houses and apartments that are usually more cramped than intimidatingly spacious, places that are rented, bought or borrowed from previous inhabitants, where lives are layered, one upon the next. We build our homes by reworking somebody else's, making the best of what we have, adjusting a space to suit our habits and needs.

Architecture is about the understanding of the world and turning it into a more meaningful and humane place.
Juhani Pallasmaa

We spill out of our homes to hygge together in public places. Taking a rug to a local park creates a small space within an open area. Spreading it out beneath a tree immediately invites shelter. Regardless of the scale of a landscape, we are not diminished in the natural world but part of it. Nature is an important part of life for many Danes.

We still carry within us, in a small warm spot, the idea of home. Home as a safe place, a loving place and a creative place. A place of comfort and privacy. A place where we can explore our inner life.

Ilse Crawford

Home

Although it's not tied to a particular setting, hygge is strongly associated with our sense of home – both the pleasure of being in a safe and welcoming environment and the serenity of being at home within ourselves.

The yearning for a safe home runs through our experience of territory, nationality, family, to our interior lives. Inside each of us are memories, fantasies and desires for home – a shelter waiting to be built, a place of peace to be revisited.

Home is an emotional state, a place in the imagination where feelings of security, belonging, placement, family, protection, memory, and personal history abide.

Thomas Moore

The home is ideally a place of solace that restores and sustains us. Home may be a particular setting or a momentary realization of a warm and protected experience that satisfies the heart. It is a place that we return to when we hygger.

Homeyness is closely aligned with hygge. It describes an idealized feeling of being at home and meets our desire to create a cosy, safe environment that resonates with our inner lives. Hygge too is a practice related to how we create and preserve meaning in the places we inhabit, how we make homes that comfort us and bring us together. Homemaking is a hyggelig experience in itself. Making beds, watering plants or laying a fire all give intimate focus to our daily lives. When we hygger we arrange ourselves and our surroundings to facilitate connection; we very deliberately situate ourselves. Then we begin to really inhabit a place or a moment in time and open ourselves to what it has to give. Hygge is a sense that we deserve to belong in our setting, that we can make it our own and in doing so, dwell in it. It is the experience of dwelling that gives us the sense of cosiness that most people refer to when they describe hygge.

Hygge shares the qualities of sheltering and security that we associate with home, but it isn't tied to property. It's a felt experience of sanctuary that takes shape in passing moments.

For years, home has been idealized as a refuge from the world, somewhere predictable and unchanging. But home isn't just where we go to escape the world. Home is how we inhabit the world. Meaning comes from connection and a willingness to pay attention to the particulars of our lives, from the things we choose to use to our daily rituals and shared activities.

All really inhabited space bears the essence of the notion of home.

Gaston Bachelard

How we spend our time in our most private sphere – cooking together, enjoying a meal, playing cards, poking a fire or watching a film – is a benchmark for how to hygge. But for many of us home is not a reliably fixed location to retreat to. Few can afford to own their own properties, and ownership is perhaps losing its appeal. Millions of people have nowhere to call home.

Without a home, everything is fragmentation.

John Berger

Although home still represents stability in an unstable world, we're beginning to see that home can be how we live, a situation that we create and recreate. Home is less attached to bricks and mortar and more about the lives we lead, the ways that we connect with each other, the communities we build. Home is a state of mind, something we make for ourselves wherever we can. Hygge is the home we make in the flux and flow of our lives. If we are fortunate enough to enjoy a place of physical and psychological safety, we can hygge and share the benefits with those around us.

Home from home

Hygge helps us rekindle home in a rented apartment in an unfamiliar city, or in a tent in the lee of a mountain. We can recall home in the cabin of a boat or tucked into an armchair beside the window in a coffee shop. Some of us are most at home sleeping under the stars. When we travel far from home, it is carried with us in small gestures – in the way we unpack our belongings in hotel rooms, wrap a blanket around our shoulders on a long bus ride or listen to a favourite tune.

Many Danes enjoy the benefit of time spent in rented summerhouses beside the sea or inland lakes. The dream of a cabin; of a small, simple place somewhere, just large enough to enclose and shelter us, speaks to both our primal need for shelter and to our changing ideas of home. It helps us to envisage how we might shed the weight of our possessions, edit our lives and discover the freedom of being together uninhibited by status and stuff. People are occasionally choosing to leave their offices and fixed accommodation in favour of a more nomadic lifestyle. With a van, a lantern, occasional WiFi and a sleeping bag, almost anywhere can feel like home.

Many of us regularly visit places to relax and reward ourselves between the challenge of work and the reality of home. These are usually settings that provide a sense of 'home from home', that offer a friendly reception, warmth, shelter, comfort and care that we don't necessarily have to reciprocate – a local pub or café. We're encouraged by the presence of others there, even if we are not interacting with them. We can lose ourselves in a state of comfortable inter-being with everyone who has come to enjoy the same experience.

Some places afford more hygge than others – we feel comfortable if we know that each one of us is welcome to inhabit a space in our own way; if we can shift the degree of privacy afforded to us and withdraw or participate at will; if the boundaries of our temporary shelter are porous enough to invite interaction, but firm enough to keep others at a comfortable distance.

Technology has liberated us to work from home but also from a bar stool or local library. Despite the privilege of being able to remain in our private domains, people are still choosing to come together, to meet to drink coffee, to eat and work and play. We need the hygge that takes place in a piazza or park. We thrive on the reassurance of each other's presence and in the security of the shelters that we build together when we hygger.

3. Comfort

Hygge involves comfort,
cosiness, a sense of wellbeing,
and a relaxed frame of mind.

Judith Friedman Hansen

Hygge is the basic language of comfort, a vernacular
common to us all, and the way that we seek comfort
is one of the foundational elements of cultures
worldwide. Every culture has a vocabulary of scent,
texture, taste, sight and sound that speaks to the
hearts and bodies of its people. Every family's life is
lined with memories, keepsakes, habits and traditions
that we draw on for sustenance. For comfort we turn
to the scripts that we have inherited. We recall and
revisit the places and people that make us feel whole
and happy.

Associations with comfort are unique to each of us, but we find a commonality in the neutral, non-verbal vocabulary of hygge that satisfies our longings for predictability, warmth, cosiness and fellow feeling, wherever we find ourselves.

Hygge happens when we acknowledge those things to which we naturally give special consideration and when we create opportunities to savour them – in pockets of ease that we create, in moments of relaxation and peacefulness. If we apply the principle of caring for ourselves and each other to our surroundings and the concrete particulars of how we live, we attune ourselves to the possibility of hygge. The secret to hygge lies in paying attention to the rhythm of our daily lives, the people we choose to spend time with, the things we use and the activities we undertake that give life value and meaning.

Hygge is an interaction between daily practice, everyday artefacts and symbols of care. Like a familiar song on the radio, heard in the car over the hum of the engine, the comfort of hygge is evanescent but very real.

Elevating the everyday

In Denmark, hygge is something consciously practised in many everyday lives, something commonplace but rarely taken for granted. It's associated with the comfort of routine and everyday ritual. Like placing a lit candle in the centre of the dinner table before a meal, it's a practice that is both concrete and abstract. It sits on the intersection between material and symbolic activity. Even the smallest action that comforts us and speaks to our hearts is part of the vocabulary of hygge.

The true secret of happiness lies in taking a genuine interest in all the details of daily life.

William Morris

Using the context and stuff of our daily lives to create an atmosphere of comfort prepares the ground for moments of unexpected intimacy and pleasure to flourish. The meals that we eat together, our workplace coffee breaks, bedtime routines, even housework, can be transformed into restorative rituals. They are an opportunity to enter a different level of everyday experience that is both soulful and practical.

The simple things that we do every day have resonance and ritual. In mundane tasks like sweeping our doorstep to welcome a guest, we clear a passageway to those times when activity gives way to contentment and ease. We can move more happily through our busy lives by being aware of the value of routine chores, enjoying some of them as small epiphanies strung through our day where we find ourselves comforted and our sense of purpose restored.

It isn't easy in our complicated world to enjoy the pleasures of ordinary living – children, family, neighbourhood, nature, walking, gathering, eating together. I imagine life not as an ambitious quest, but as an anti-quest, a search for the ordinary and a cultivation of the unexceptional.

Thomas Moore

The comfort of the familiar

Hygge favours predictability and ordinariness, excluding it from events marked by uncertainty. Like a sense of home, hygge is an experience that no one can take away from us. It blooms in our reminiscence and thrives in familiar places and the stability of old habits. It's hygge that we seek in the encircling charm of a favourite armchair or a particular pile of books beside our bed. We achieve hygge with practice by beginning with the things that are familiar and comforting to us, like a grandmother's recipe that we prepare and then savour alone or share with others, with the table laid and the fire lit.

Danes learn how to hygge in early childhood. Although it's a skill that is never overtly taught, their lives are infused with it. Learning the language of hygge is like a game played in the playground. None of the rules have been clearly explained but each child simply joins in and absorbs the rhythm of the game as they play. Hygge isn't complicated and there are no impenetrable regulations. It depends on nothing more than putting down our baggage and wholeheartedly stepping into the game.

Comforting each other

To comfort each other, we share gestures and recipes for happiness associated with home as simple as putting a blanket around someone's shoulders or making a bowl of chicken soup.

We cannot all do great things. But we can do small things with great love.

Mother Teresa

Hygge is like a harmony that breathes its way around a place while you light a fire, hold hands in a warm, dark cinema or make tea. It's a celebration of ease and wellbeing that affects everyone present until we all move to the same rhythm, adapted to relaxation and peacefulness. It sings out against other factors that shape our lives; the tread of a nine-to-five job, the stress of a disharmonious relationship or an afternoon spent alone with a fractious baby.

The way that we hygger and offer reassurance is unique to each one of us according to the things to which we attach most meaning. Some of us nourish others by cooking. Some offer comfort in conversation or good-natured humour. Others are adept at creating an easy ambience through which hygge flows.

When we hygger we create an environment where we can be close to one another. A nest of mattresses pushed together beside a fire or two chairs set side by side on a balcony are enough to invite togetherness. Hygge satisfies our creaturely needs. The proximity of another body is primal comfort. Intimacy and the experience of feeling in touch with our surroundings characterize a hyggelig moment. We feel the caressing embrace of the space and people around us. Like animals returning to the familiar texture of a lair, we relax more easily in an enclosed, softly illuminated place.

How we need that security. How we need another soul to cling to, another body to keep us warm. To rest and trust; to give your soul in confidence: I need this. I need someone to pour myself into.

Sylvia Plath

Hygge helps us to create an environment that supports the needs of our hearts and provides room for human experience. It is important to hygge around someone who is sad. Through hygge we can explore the subtlety of empathy. Danes are not characteristically gushing or hysterical. Their talent for providing the uncomplicated solace of hygge proves that it's possible to live life in touch with emotion without resorting to over sentimentality.

Expressing love by doing small things is part of the vocabulary of hygge, like preparing a lover's favourite dish, putting a hot water bottle between cold sheets, wrapping a gift with particular care. Hygge is the spirit in which we give and receive.

Welcome

Danes experience an overall sense of comfort wherever they are in their homeland. Like so much in Danish culture, welcome is implied. As a result, they meet newcomers in subtle acknowledgment rather than effusive demonstrations of greeting. On occasion visitors to Denmark perceive Danes as polite but distant, but Danes are adept at creating a convivial atmosphere. Hygge extends an invitation for interaction and promises a warm reception.

Placing a lantern on a doorstep symbolizes welcome. Putting a basket of knitted slippers by our front door invites housemates and guests to shed some of their discomfort, tread softly and clothe themselves in the unifying comfort of home.

Wrapped together in the Danish word *omsorg*, caring for, are the notions of solicitude, attention and concern. *Omsorg* describes the sense of being provided for. It's an expression of welcome and commitment that is closely bound to the creation of a hyggelig experience, revealed in thoughtful gestures like picking flowers to put on a bedside table or buying a friend their preferred beer before they reach the bar. This consideration is usually associated with the role of a host who smoothes our concerns and insecurities with their ease and calm attention, but it's a quality of care that we can provide for ourselves by indulging in small luxuries, like fresh flowers, a lie-in with a new book or enjoying a glass of wine at the end of a long day at work.

Coming to our senses

Hygge is a sensory experience. It reconciles us with the world by engaging our emotions and our senses.

When we hygger we allow the materiality of our
bodies to become bound up with the physical qualities
of our surroundings, and we pay attention to the
needs of our hearts.

Visible and mobile, my body
is a thing among things; it's
caught in the fabric of the world,
and its cohesion is that of a
thing. But, because it moves
itself and sees, it holds things
in a circle around itself.

Maurice Merleau-Ponty

A hyggelig experience is protected, controlled,
personal and intimate. It echoes the embrace of
home. Most of us instinctively recognize the comfort
of a hyggeligt environment when we step into one
but don't always have a clear idea of how it has been
accomplished. There is no formula, no sum of obvious
material parts to be slotted together, but if we create
conditions that appeal to our senses, we ground

ourselves in the moment and harness hygge. An initial step to creating hygge is to give thought to the textures, sounds, scents and tastes of our lives, to the quality of materiality that surrounds us.

Home should be a warm, liveable place that is alive, a place to please the eye and soothe the senses in scale, curves, colour, variety, pattern and texture.

Josef Frank

The design of our homes, workplaces and public spaces has been dominated in recent years by how they look, with insufficient attention given to how they feel. When we hygger, we focus on atmosphere and good materials to make changes to shift that imbalance.

To comfort each other, we acknowledge the importance of emotion. Since the dominant logic of the Industrial Revolution, incorporating sentiment and soul into the design of our lives has been dismissed as light and feminine, but Danish material culture has always celebrated both human feeling and the nurturing presence of the natural world. The tender values embedded in Danish society and a love of nature have encouraged Danish designers to combine sensuality, emotion and robust practicality with an awareness of the materiality that connects us and the objects that we use. In Denmark, design evolved with a distinctly warm, natural and human touch, combined with the pared back simplicity of Modernism.

...the problem is this: how do you measure wellbeing, happiness, tactility, trust, freedom, friendship, awareness, beauty, love, memory and so on?

Ilse Crawford

In addition to embracing the mechanization of the industrial era, Scandinavians sought to preserve their national identities and resist the departure of tradition. They took pains to sustain rural crafts and customary skills. In acknowledgement of rural culture they drew inspiration from peasant farmhouses – multifunctional single-room, timber-framed structures with simple practical furnishings. These evolved into the airy living spaces filled with the sensual shapes, handcrafted goods, understated comfort, warmth and light that we associate with Scandinavian design today.

Warmth

The essence of comfort must be a handful of people warming themselves by a fire and enjoying each other's proximity. Perhaps this ancient assurance, common to all cultures, is the origin of hygge. Danes link warmth with goodness. The common symbols of hygge – a fireplace, candlelight, newly baked buns and hot chocolate – all suggest warmth.

A hearth is a place of peace and a source of energy. It represents the comfort of heat, heart, protection and food. The Latin word for hearth, fireplace, flame or central point is *focus*. The primary focal point in most Danish homes is the hearth – now separated into kitchens, open fires and wood-burning stoves. Through dark winters and a love of home and hospitality, Scandinavians have held on to a culture of warmth. The hearth remains the symbolic centre of the home, a place to gather, to prepare warming food and to hygge.

The primal attraction of an open fire or wood-burning stove speaks to our hearts and radiates a warmth that is very different from central heating; it lifts and soothes our spirits. In Danish homes fireplaces were never meant to be ornate centrepieces, but functional and focal points. They are often found in the corner of a room, radiating hygge. Today, many Danes don't have the luxury of a fireplace but they instinctively make up for it by burning candles and paying careful attention to how they light their homes, using subdued lighting or *dæmpet belysning*, to accompany hygge.

In trying to translate hygge, people point to candlelight as if it can illuminate the meaning of the word. The meaning and message of candlelight is the ultimate symbol of hygge but it doesn't contain it; it communicates and enhances it. Candles on a table symbolize that we have chosen to sit together, not simply to satiate our hunger, but to enjoy a hyggelig time.

The Danish expression *levende lys* (living light) describes the comfort of a dancing flame – something warm, alive, authentic and linked to the spreading of hygge. Throughout Scandinavia, candles are lit on windowsills through the darkest months of the year. The sight of living light in a place ignites the assumption that hygge abides there. If a naked flame is an alarming prospect, a candle set into a lantern is a reassuring alternative. In the absence of living light, choosing to supplement the functional lighting of our homes with lamps that glow softly alludes to the warmth of a flame and still offers the caress of shadow on the periphery.

When we hygger, we feel encircled by warmth. Sometimes it is found in each other's company, sometimes the heat of a stove or the embracing glow of a circle of lamplight just sufficient to illuminate a gathering around a table. There is comfort in being alone in a warm bed, the luxury of a deep bath or sitting in companionable silence with a friend in the evening sun. Hygge is an experience of warmth, inside and out; good company, a comfortable location, a hot drink, a blanket, being held, being fed.

Danes simply know how to hygge. It is bred in their bones. Like growing up with love, if we are fortunate enough to be exposed to hygge for long enough, it changes life. The spirit of hygge is spread by warm-heartedness and generosity. We can light a thousand candles but the flame of hygge is easily extinguished by a mean spirit.

If the concept of hygge exists outside the realm of our experience, that doesn't mean it will always be unavailable. It only takes one match or a single kind gesture to illuminate the dark.

Touch

Touch pulls us into the present moment, calms our minds and bodies. When we hygger we are aware of what touches us daily, we consider the textures that surround us and consciously take comfort from the fabric of our lives – from the clothes that we wear to the way that we furnish our homes. We gather materials around us that awaken our senses, and combine them to clothe us in comfort. The softness of a hyggelig experience draws us in, holds and reveals us. It allows comfort to flow between us and into the spaces we inhabit.

Danes prefer to live with natural materials that have honesty and integrity, materials that wear well and feel good to touch. The most common building material is wood, left unvarnished to allow its warmth and patterns to breathe. Wood is a living substance that invites us to touch it. Danes combine it with the solidity and richness of stone, brick, copper and concrete, also left unadorned for tactile appeal. Our sensitivity to raw materials encourages us to linger. Wooden floors, sisal matting or woollen carpets underfoot feel warm and welcoming. A space softened with textiles offers us an entry point into a world of comfort that we can each experience as our own. When we take ownership of a space, we feel the comfort of its human qualities that nurture us and keep us feeling safe and happy.

O for a life of Sensations rather than of Thoughts.

John Keats

Fresh, clean sheets on a bed of down, linen and cotton, the comforting weight of a good blanket or the primal appeal of a sheepskin thrown over a chair all touch us and ask us to stop and hygge. Hygge is the comfort of soft woollen socks, the sturdy cosiness of woven fabric, the smoothness of felt. It's the feeling of warm sun on our faces, sand between our toes, a round stone in a pocket, the warmth of a hand. Hygge is sliding into bed in the winter to find a patch of cat-warmth by our feet. Vintage textiles softened and worn with use, quilts patched with love, a basket of blankets arranged so that anyone can envelop themselves in warmth. The portable, sensuous luxury of a cashmere scarf, a wrap placed around our shoulders, the gift of a blanket to be carried from room to room or taken on long journeys.

All credibility, all good conscience, all evidence of truth come only from the senses.

Friedrich Nietzsche

Our clothes hold us in their creases and folds. Cotton and wool soothe our skin and allow it to breathe. Clothes that are designed for comfort and practicality mean that we can move without inhibition. When we want to hygge, we often change or discard clothes, finding woolen jumpers or pyjamas, shrugging off a jacket, loosening ties.

The grace of a curve is an invitation to remain. We cannot break away from it without hoping to return.

Gaston Bachelard

Curves hold a sense of enclosure. The things that we touch comfort us if they curve beneath our palms

– a wooden bowl, the arm of a chair, the slope of a shoulder. Our bodies take refuge in the familiar corners and curves that give us a sense of ease and pause.

We curve around each other for comfort. Hygge is the intimacy of proximity. When we curl up together on a sofa or climb into bed, touching each other's bodies, we know the primal pleasure of contact with warm skin.

Hygge is enhanced by the embrace of furniture created for privacy and togetherness. Deep corner sofas that invite us to sit in, not on, them are made for contact, comfort and relaxation. They encourage us to lounge and play. Our bodies need space to move. A bed big enough for the whole family, beanbags and floor cushions, mean both the freedom to wriggle and the luxury of nearness. The touch of a well-designed dining chair supporting our back relaxes us and holds us happily around the table late into the night. Classic Danish elliptical coffee tables and round tables draw us towards each other. The egalitarian design of benches and settles affords us the opportunity to be close to each other, bringing us together.

Certain things make us feel safe – the embrace of a high-backed chair, the sound as we pull a wooden door to a close. An extra chair swiftly found to accommodate an unexpected guest makes them feel wanted. Danes prefer lightweight and mobile furniture that can be easily rearranged to ensure comfort and contact.

Scent
Scent can transport us instantly to the comfort of the past; it is our sense of smell that is most strongly linked to our emotions. Moments of reassurance can be swiftly conjured up by a particular scent. Maybe it's the aroma of good cigar smoke, the smell of melting butter or shoe polish, wet dogs or washing powder. Perhaps it's newly mown grass, jasmine, wood shavings, old books or chamomile. The pleasure that we recall is as individual as the lives we lead.

Nothing awakens a reminiscence like an odour.
Victor Hugo

Hygge can be swiftly evoked or dispelled by scent. The comfort of hygge is usually associated with cleanliness. Walking into a house heavy with unfamiliar perfumes is not hyggelig. Neither are unwashed bodies, dirty washing or places that smell of neglect. In Denmark, a home that smells clean and natural is considered inviting. Danes often buy flowers, brew coffee, make cakes. Hygge is caught in an armful of washing gathered from a line that smells of fresh air and sunshine. It's in the smell of herbs grown outside a backdoor, fragrant food, newly baked bread and fresh air. It lingers in wood smoke and the recognizably warm scents of vanilla and musk. And hygge is found in the familiar smell of someone we love.

Listen

There is a quiet pulse at the heart of hygge that cannot be heard through a cacophony of noise. To feel wrapped in the comfort of sound, we need to be able to discern what we hear.

Hygge is a quality of engagement. When we hygger, we want to be able to hear each other, to be in a position where we can remain on our own frequency or tune in and out of each other's at will. Domestic appliances that call for our attention, or the interruption of electronic notifications that pull us away from the moment or from each other, detract from a hyggelig experience. Unexpected or unwelcome noise like the screech of a siren or a door slammed in the early hours of the morning pull us away from our sphere of comfort.

Natural sound is universally comforting: rain on a roof, light wind, bird song, the crackling of an open fire. Or the sound of a lover's heartbeat. The noise of life going on around us – such as the voices of our neighbours over a fence or the sound of someone preparing food in our kitchen – ensures that we do not feel alone. The reassuring honk of geese returning home, the sound of a spade turning the soil, the roll and hum of a train.

We are all attracted to different levels of sound. For some of us hygge is evoked by music or the bustle of a busy street. For others it is found in the solace of silence. The chatter of diners enjoying themselves in a restaurant is hyggelig. A strident or loud individual is not. Discordant voices create imbalance and dispel the fragile magic of hygge. Hygge is dependent on a stability of presence, and even tone.

Nourish

Sharing a meal is the epitome of hygge. It brings us together, nourishing our bodies and spirits. In Denmark, food has always been connected to tradition and time spent with family and friends. Shared meals are part of the rhythm of Danish everyday life.

Households gather around a table at the end of most working days to eat together. Many colleagues stop work to enjoy lunch at the same time. These are the moments when rich connections are made. Sitting together to eat is one of the few occasions when we talk to, listen to and entertain each other, sharing confidences and ideas. It can be a time to taste and deepen our understanding of another culture.

After a good dinner one can forgive anybody, even one's own relations.

Oscar Wilde

Every society has traditions connected to food. We carry them with us through recipes, ritual and habit. Asking our fathers and grandmothers for the ingredients and instructions for meals that have brought us comfort in the past, and preparing them for the people we love, links one culture and one generation to the next. Comfort food is particularly hyggelig. Each one of us knows the restorative pleasure of eating something that we associate with love and care. There isn't much self-deprivation in

Denmark; Danes are kind to themselves. They eat well, in moderation, and afford each other the same consideration and generosity.

Every repast can have soul and can be enchanting; it asks for only a small degree of mindfulness and a habit of doing things with care and imagination.

Thomas Moore

The love that we put into preparing food changes its nature, and the way that food is served enhances the experience. Hygge flows out of the kitchen in small gestures such as warming plates and bowls in the oven before serving a meal, and making even a simple meal look appetizing by arranging it carefully on the plate. Taking time to set an inviting table to gather around for a meal, or even a snack, transforms eating into sharing. An old tablecloth and tea lights in jam jars can transform an ordinary occasion into an experience that holds us together long after the candles have been

blown out. Paying attention to detail and not keeping ingredients, crockery or glasses for special occasions, but using the best of what we have, elevates the meals that we eat every day.

A typical informal Danish lunch of smørrebrød is prepared in advance so that everyone can help themselves, sit down together and enjoy the meal at their leisure. The ritual order in which the food is enjoyed, and the frequent pauses to toast in appreciation of the host, elevates an everyday meal to a moment of hygge.

We all contribute to the success of a meal. Each one of us brings something to the table; an idea, a custom or just the pleasure that we express in the opportunity to be fed. In Denmark, food is a shared indulgence. Danes wholeheartedly give themselves over to the pleasure of eating. Obvious restraint is incompatible with hygge. Guests are urged to give in to temptation. Hosts are openhanded and generous. The food provided is seen as a luxury to be enjoyed. Everyone is encouraged to believe that a measure of pleasure beats abstinence, and that it's a shame to remove oneself from life's simple joys. The Danish tendency to happily permit self-indulgence in small amounts, eating a few rather than totally abstaining, contributes to the hygge around a table.

If you bake bread with indifference, you bake a bitter bread that feeds but half man's hunger.

Kahlil Gibran

Buying food with thought and preparing it with care gives us an opportunity to slow down, to engage all our senses, to nourish ourselves. There is a new appetite for sensual, pleasure-giving food in Scandinavia. Qualities currently associated with Nordic food are freshness, simplicity and ethics. New Nordic Cuisine places emphasis on ingredients that are locally sourced, that are typical of a region's climate, soil and water. It is inspired rather than restricted by using only seasonal produce, and has revived old techniques like smoking, salting and marinating. It promotes conscious consumption and animal welfare by relying on production that is in harmony with the local, natural resources in fields, the sea and in the wild. And it has introduced many people to the solitary pleasure or communal activity of foraging.

Both hygge and New Nordic Cuisine situate us in time and place. The food expresses a land or *terroir* on a plate, and hygge pulls us into the flavour of the present moment. Both are playing a part in the wider flourishing of a community of people who are passionate about the pleasure of sharing nourishing food and are asking us to think about what we eat, to see the possibilities around us, connecting us to our local environment. A food market is a place to see the soul of the city, where people taste and celebrate life together, where hygge and community thrive in the conversations that take place around the stalls.

See

When we hygger, we are mindful of detail. We pay attention to our needs and to those of others. We notice and appreciate the things that have been prepared or put aside for our comfort – a well-laid fire, a clean bath towel at the end of a bed, a pillow put on the passenger seat for a long journey. And we see and address the small omissions that collectively combine to diminish the quality of an experience or place. To enjoy hygge there needs to be a certain harmony, a balance of form, light and shade, texture and space. Haphazard assembly and carelessness are the opposite of the practical mindfulness that characterizes hygge. Although control is the antithesis of hygge, mess and too much disorder diminish the likelihood that it will appear.

Neither meticulousness nor messiness in a room are hyggelig, but the organized disorder of a home which is being lived in can be.

Judith Friedman Hansen

Hygge is reflected in clean surfaces. It is lovingly folded into clothes or a handwritten note, revealed in the small signs that show we care. Subtle hints of wear comfort us. A worn leather sofa or the soft folds of an old jumper communicate ease and invite relaxation. A complicitous smile or the sight of someone we love is hygge. When we step across a threshold to be greeted by familiar faces, objects, silhouettes and shadows, we know that we are home.

Simple, sensual shapes that echo forms in the natural world, and arrangements that allude to domestic space, flood us with feelings of familiarity and comfort. Certain things exude hygge, particularly those with a rounded appearance and warm colours. They seem to have a quality of homeyness to them that radiates out into the world, inviting us to touch, hold and use them again and again. Things that are unadorned speak of the authenticity and accessibility that we seek in hygge. Danes value lack of pretension and appreciate homes that appear to be striving to be no more or no less equal to the house next door.

Informality

A hyggeligt environment presents itself without defence or artifice, to reassure anyone who steps inside that they can forgo affectation and formality. It is accessible and immediate, unselfconsciously arranged, but clean and well kept. It feels lived in, informal and relaxed. Hygge puts us at our ease, reassuring us that no particular demeanour or posture is expected of us. We can be ourselves without risk of embarrassment, and open to spontaneity. When we hygger, we create a civil, joyful and non-challenging environment, a place where everyone feels at home.

Imperfection

There is comfort in imperfection, in well-worn clothes, lived in places and unpretentious people. The new and unused feel distant and self-conscious, lacking the history of relation that comes with time.

Perfection is not hyggelig, newness is not hyggelig.

Judith Friedman Hansen

Hygge is about care and attention to detail but not about constraint. Perfectionism inhibits hygge, makes us hold our breath and tightens the atmosphere around us. Hygge recoils from premeditated order and uniformity; it has to be allowed to manifest organically. For the spirit of hygge to come to a home or an occasion, things need to be lovingly put in place and then released. We must be prepared to let go of our expectations and allow hygge to flow softly through our environment. When we invite people into our homes, they need to feel free to inhabit the space in their own way. A matrix of unspoken

rules and resentments leaves a gathering confused
and taut.

Hygge is a celebration of the spontaneous
and honest, a step towards a life that is real
and uncontrived. It can't be summoned by the
arrangement of a perfect scene or engineered by
a carefully styled table. The essence of hygge is
contained in the seeds of our intentions, and it will
flourish or wither according to how generously those
seeds are planted. Hygge is a fragile bloom that can't
be forced. It often thrives in the unpredictable and
imperfect conditions on the margins, where there is
space for it to grow unhindered and unobserved –
the scruffy restaurant in a back street, or a friend's
quiet apartment.

The stuff of life

The way that a space is filled and contained holds
our lives in a reassuring embrace. Situating ourselves
within a comfortable sphere of knowable and
sensuous objects feels hyggelig. There is a mutual
adjustment between people and things that takes
place when we hygger, a recognition and settling that
affords ease and peace of mind, like the way we nestle

into an armchair at the end of a long day, move a table closer to the fire in a local pub or wrap our hands around a favourite mug.

The things of this world are vessels, entrances for stories; when we touch them or tumble into them, we fall into their labyrinthine resonances.

Lynda Sexson

Some things seem to afford an intuitive usability – a pair of scissors or an old garden fork that we always choose above any other, that needs to be bent into shape each time but remains irresistible. Or the rocking chair that seems to keep us company as we soothe a baby back to sleep in the lonely, early morning hours. There are things that we feel inexorably drawn to. The same pair of creased leather shoes, a scratched, orange melamine bowl, a well-thumbed book of poetry. We often reach for particular kitchen utensils; a wooden spoon, a spatula burnt and worn smooth

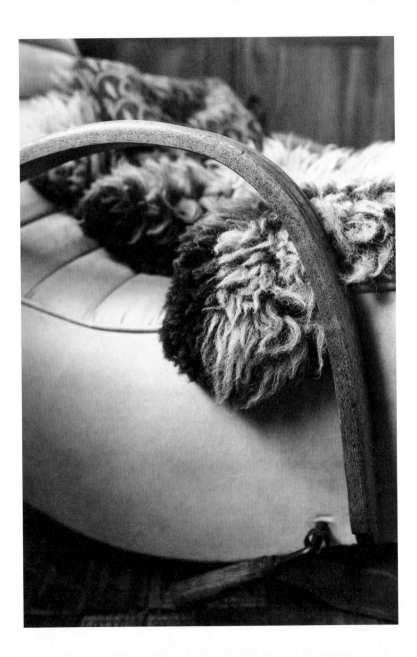

along one edge but used time and time again. Those are the things with which we feel compatible that contribute a sense of order in our minds and speak to our hearts. Each one provides its own measure of hygge to our daily lives by evoking primal associations of pleasure, comfort and safety.

We live and the things around us live, through daily care.

Ilse Crawford

Hygge is a quality of engagement and care. The quiet ordering of things can place us and reveal us. A Dane will often pair objects together. Two candlesticks on a sideboard or matching plants on a windowsill may subtly allude to immaterial aspects of Danish culture such as balance and equality. Each one of us appropriates things to express our own identity – some of us stick postcards to the fridge, others put beach stones on a windowsill or paperweights on a desk.

A pile of books beside a bed is hyggelig like a reliable group of old friends or a gentle acknowledgment of the person that we would like to become one day. It is in climbing into bed early to read those books and in carefully tending to the stuff of our lives that we hygger.

To create a hyggeligt environment we pay more attention to balance and harmony than to display. We give things space to breathe and a specific context that particularizes them, ensuring that each item contributes its measure of comfort with presence and purpose.

Things sing when they reach a certain degree of presence.

Thomas Moore

When we hygger we consciously connect to and share the stuff of our lives. Hygge is not about accumulating household goods to engineer a homey atmosphere. It is communicated by what we do, not by what we have. A hyggelig space is for relatedness, for sharing not showing off. If we consider and care for each object that we keep, we become producers of meaning rather than consumers of goods. Ultimately, hygge is not about the stuff of our lives but the way we live.

Memory

The things around us contain our stories and invite connection and conversation. Each home contains a symbolic ecology of objects and totems that speak of the lives of its inhabitants. Each one of us finds meaning in things that represent our actions, goals, achievements and the salient events of our lives. The things that we keep comfort us; concrete symbols of the life we have led. Everyday life is held together by the strands of meaning that loved and worn items convey.

Memory is an imaginal constellation of past and present that generates a new experience. Memory is not the storing of the past, but the storying of the present.

Lynda Sexson

Most of us can single out a handful of things that give order to what we have experienced, and when we see them we feel that past and present are related. The meaning of our private lives is tethered to a few objects – a book inherited from a friend, a photograph of our grandparents' farm, a wooden box that we have made ourselves.

Books that have been given to us, inscribed and dated and handmade gifts speak of our personal ties. Our children's artworks delight us with their enduring vitality, and remind us of how swiftly time passes. Snapshots capture moments of pleasure. Heirlooms remind us of our heritage. In our appreciation of a well-turned bowl or delicate watercolour, we participate in its creation. It becomes part of a shared history. Paintings can take us back to a particular place, to a café in a Parisian square or a baobab tree under a wide African sky.

The ephemera and scraps of the ordinary world that find their way into our pockets – a fossil found on a windy beach, a rusted bottle top or a porcupine quill – remind us of the transitory beauty of our lives. Our souvenirs and mementos are a material way of situating us with respect to time. This temporal emplacement, the interplay between past and present, is important to many Danes. It provides a sense of valued continuity. *Minde*, or keepsakes, are an important element of a Danish home, particularly

for older generations. *At mindes* means to bring something back into our thoughts, to recall memories, atmosphere and associations. Danes enjoy restorative nostalgia and have an affection for heirlooms, knowledge of Danish history and family genealogy. They have a rich awareness of how to furnish their lives with known traditions and treasured occasions. A Dane will often reminisce about particularly enjoyable moments characterized by the warmth and pleasurable togetherness of hygge.

Hygge gives us a place in time that is defined and easy to recall. It holds past and present together. When we hygger, we frame the moment, give it our full attention, savour and hold it, in an awareness that the moment will pass. We feel how one moment becomes layered on to the next; past and present mingled together – everything falling into place, into one accord.

We do not remember days, we remember moments.

Cesare Pavese

4. Wellbeing

Wellbeing is about a deep rapport with ourselves and the world around us. Hygge strengthens that rapport by nurturing consideration, responsiveness and delight in our relationships with the places we inhabit and the people who make up our families and communities. It is an integral part of the wholesome, balanced life many of us associate with Denmark.

The feeling of wellbeing that we experience when we hygger can't be measured or stretched into statistics to support the well-known fact that the Danes are some of the happiest people in the world. There is a bedrock of contentment beneath everyday life in Denmark that is more stable than the waves of happiness that flow above it.

Contentment

In Denmark, people are quietly confident that life is good. Their basic needs are met, their material expectations modest. The country is historically homogeneous and Danes feel that they belong to their country and to each other, dwelling happily in their gentle, predictable surroundings, trusting and safe. There is still very little uncertainty or pressure from their environment, and a minimum amount of essential authority to constrain them. They have a strong societal conscience and the way that they downplay social difference and economic disparity creates an even tone to daily life. Although Danes share many concerns with the rest of the world, and complaining about high taxes, media and government is a pastime, the majority are happy to contribute to a system that efficiently supports their uncomplicated way of life and facilitates the opportunity to enjoy wellbeing.

He who knows contentment is rich.

Lao Tzu

Because of their common heritage, Danes have often been viewed as a tribe rather than a complex nation. Although the structure of Danish society has been enriched in recent years with the arrival of migrant populations, Danish culture still exhibits the distinct characteristics of self-reliance, solidarity and few disparities that come from their roots in ancient rural communities. Historically, lack of internal conflict has facilitated wellbeing. The emblem of hygge represents the sense of belonging, togetherness and joie de vivre that seems to bind the whole nation.

A happy life must be to a great extent a quiet life, for it is only in an atmosphere of quiet that true joy can live.

Bertrand Russell

The Danish expression *man vil hinanden*, we intend each other, suggests a combination of kinship and benevolence, and expresses the pleasure that we take in the comfort of one another's appealing presence.

The contentment we feel when we walk down our local street, stopping to talk to familiar passersby, is hygge; to experience a sense of intimacy and basic trust in the good intentions of others. We can hygge together or alone, with strangers in a bar, at home or at work, inside or outside, wherever we feel a sense of being known or simply at peace with ourselves and others.

Livskunst, the art of living, describes the things we do to create a life of authenticity and wellbeing. Hygge is a life art. It captures a way of being with other people, caring for them and for ourselves. When we hygger we prepare the ground for relationships to thrive. The art of hygge is contained in many small actions that go together to manifest the whole, like turning the soil before putting a plant in the ground, soaking it in water so that it is softened and ready, gently teasing out the roots, digging a hole deep enough to contain it, adding compost to suit its habitat, bedding it in, watering it, talking to it, then watching it grow and flourish.

To become fluent in the language of hygge we begin with the idea that we are connected and that a window has opened for us to feel good. If we are in company we want each other to experience warmth, to share, to communicate, to be together, to feel part of a greater whole, and to know that we are shielded from disquiet and difficulty, just for a while. Hygge offers a break in things, a brief, content, restorative pause.

I have never looked upon ease and happiness as ends in themselves – such an ethical basis I call more proper for a herd of swine. The ideals that have lighted me on my way and time after time given me new courage to face life cheerfully, have been Truth, Goodness, and Beauty.

Albert Einstein

Optimism

There are many threads that weave together to form the fabric of wellbeing in Denmark, and one of them is a readiness to see life from a positive perspective. Danes regularly express gratitude and satisfaction without lacquering it in mawkish sentiment. They give value to the richness of everyday life. Instead of pursuing happiness as a goal, they see it as a way of being, something to actively work at each day by making the most of little things, such as chatting to a friend, slipping feet into a pair of warm socks or dancing alone in the kitchen.

If we make an effort to stay in love with life itself by cultivating contentment, we engender wellbeing. Our methods are unique to each of us. Maybe it is singing with our children in the car on the way to school or drinking coffee alone in a warm kitchen at dawn. It is in the immediacy and spontaneity of small events that hygge is found. An atmosphere of contentment and subtle joyfulness depends on our willingness to give ourselves over to an occasion with positive attention and a minimum of self-conscious reserve, even if there is no one but us to savour the moment.

Hygge is a theme that can be lived in the middle of all the other elements of an engaged life. It's not the absence of challenge or discomfort but a way of dealing with them. When we hygger we are not ignoring difficulty, but putting it down for a while. Pain and shadow still exist on the periphery of an experience of hygge. We acknowledge their presence and prepare ourselves to address them by committing ourselves to the pleasures of the present moment, in order to regain momentum and cope with life with equanimity in the future.

Presence

Hygge is a quality of presence and openness, an entirely in-the-moment experience that entails a readiness to put distractions aside. When we hygger, we step into a fluid continuum of past, present and future. By acknowledging the past and paying attention to the present, we feel both a sense of continuity and a feeling of being anchored in the now. We let go of striving towards the future and recognize that our happiness does not consist of solid realities but of abstract feelings of wellbeing and assurance.

Both in thought and in feeling, even though time be real, to realize the unimportance of time is the gate of wisdom.

Bertrand Russell

A sense of wellbeing comes from an active engagement with the world, from cultivating small-scale happiness, like putting a chair outside to sit alone in the sun, singing in a local choir or holding hands over a dinner table. It is the value that we give to a situation that elevates it to a hyggelig moment. Once we become attuned to its patterns, we move through each day recognizing scenes that resonate with our own experience of hygge, that affirm our sense of wellbeing – passing a porch decorated with fairy lights, a couple lying in a sunlit patch of grass, even a field of cows chewing in companionable silence.

There are many ways of sharing hygge. The important thing is to subscribe to the particulars of the moment. Then everyone is held in the embrace of overall warmth, each person participating in their own way, according to their own rhythm. Some people contribute by listening, others with laughter and storytelling. We hygger in different ways, at different times – eating together, going for a slow bike ride, drinking wine by a canal or smoking alone at an open window high above a busy street. Some days, to hygge is to simply shut out distractions, lie still together in bed, saying nothing but revelling in ease and mutuality. On others, it is to walk a familiar path alone, absorbed in nothing but preserving a peaceful state of mind.

Hygge is mindfulness more akin to noticing than contemplation, a quality of stillness born of contentment and awareness. It is a feeling of connection that surfaces when we stop whirling for long enough to enter our present experience by doing something as simple as eating a piece of cake on a park bench on the way home from work, or standing on a balcony at dusk to watch rooks whiffle and drop into their nests before we prepare an evening meal.

That it will never come again is what makes life so sweet.

Emily Dickinson

Acceptance

Accepting that hygge is a fleeting enchantment and that we will have to move beyond the pleasure of the moment is almost a precondition for enjoying the experience. We don't hygge to be content, we find contentment in hygge. It is an achievement in itself.

To be so focused that we lose awareness of all the contributory elements around us is not hyggelig. We

need to hold on to our appreciation of everything
at play in the background. Hygge is not about
removing ourselves but about pleasure, presence and
participation. It's not about complete freedom but
the understanding that if we are to wholeheartedly
participate in life, we are entitled to small islands of
calm. If we only have half an hour to spare, we can still
light a candle, cradle a mug of warm tea in both hands
and read one chapter of a book. In acceptance of the
limitations that life imposes on us and in knowing that
we can choose our attitude in any given circumstance
and make the best of our situation, we throw open
the window to hygge.

Balance

Danes value balance in all areas of life. They naturally
seek equilibrium, through moderation and compromise.
In Denmark, there is an obvious balance between
modernity and tradition, capitalism and socialism,
indulgence and restraint, tolerance and teasing,
and the levelling sanctions of egalitarian values and
personal freedom.

Hygge is a way of being that naturally encourages
temperance. It is bound up with *den gyldne middelvej*,

the golden middle way, a metaphor for moderation and compromise. It is associated with preserving social balance and personal harmony.

The pragmatic Danes see compromise not as losing out but as a win-win situation where both parties come away with something. Compromise is a path to wellbeing easily oiled by the humour and conviviality associated with hygge. The Danish inclination to compromise can be seen on a political level where proportional representation usually results in coalition governments rather than single party rule. The outcome is that policy gravitates towards the middle ground and a higher number of people are satisfied.

Common sense in an uncommon degree is what the world calls wisdom.

Samuel Taylor Coleridge

In seeking a more hyggeligt life, we can choose a way of being that helps us find an appropriate work-life balance, that maintains stability of body and mind, self and society. Hygge helps us to define our own unique rhythm and to establish a life in consonance with our families and our community.

Nature

With their roots in rural landscape, Danes remain connected to the vitality and spirit of their earthly nature. They happily inhabit their bodies and live in alignment with natural rhythms, day and night, seasons and tides.

Although many Danes live in apartments, they choose to spend a significant portion of their lives outside. And they invite light and the vitality of nature into their homes by opening windows to fresh air and putting green and flowering plants on windowsills and tabletops.

Danes radiate wellbeing that comes from incidental daily contact and easy rapport with the natural world. Adults and children cycle, walk or use public transport in all weathers – enjoying the kiss of the sun or wrapping up against wind and rain between home and school or work. Gathering at a bus stop or cycling past each other on the street has informality and intimacy about it, a sense of hyggelig connection.

'Just living isn't enough,' said the butterfly, 'one must have sunshine, freedom, and a little flower.'

Hans Christian Andersen

Denmark is a small country, almost entirely surrounded by water. Distances between communities are short, and life is built to scale in harmony with the open, gentle landscape. The sea is never far away and the Danes take advantage of its proximity by spending time with their families and friends on the beach at the end of a working day in summer, even enjoying the shock of a quick, cold dip all year round. Danish cities are small. Woodland, water and open countryside meet city boundaries; no one is far from the embrace of the natural world.

Four hundred years ago, the Danish government began to offer small plots of land to industrial workers who lived in crowded urban conditions, in order that they could escape the city for fresh air and to grow food. Thousands of Danes still regularly leave city centres to spend time in these *kolonihaver* or allotments. Most contain rudimentary buildings, many with unreliable

plumbing and no electricity, but they are lovingly cared for and sought after. Hygge blooms in *Kolonihaver*, in the sense of community that grows there.

Long, cold Danish winters encourage people to gather together, light candles against the dark and hygge. But in the summer, Danes hygge together in public places, celebrating the light by spending as much time outside as possible, sitting together in gardens and parks with their faces turned to the sun. Their uncomplicated physicality and easy relationship with local nature engenders a countrywide sense of reveling in the hyggelig embrace of the natural world.

By enlivening our senses, hygge connects us to our bodies and instincts, makes us feel part of and reflective of nature. Many of us enjoy spending time tending gardens, window boxes and allotments. Weeding, digging, staking and pruning slows us down to the pace of nature and puts us in touch with the perennial cycle of growth and decay and the seasonal and diurnal rhythms that are reflected in our own beings. We find contentment and tranquillity in closely observing a flower or planting a seed, in cultivating beautiful or nourishing plants. There is hygge in the intimacy of care that we give a garden, in the way that we become intertwined with its tendrils and unique temperament and enjoy the reciprocity of a relationship with a world of living, growing, crawling, reaching things.

Hygge is found in the contrast of hearing thunder around us as we shelter inside from a storm or the sense of gathering darkness as day turns to night and we light our homes and turn inward. It is evoked by half-light in those moments of containment bracketed by the rising or setting sun. It is held in the fold of a landscape or the fire that we light beneath a wide night sky.

Hygge is the anticipation of a warm fire at the end of a winter walk, the sight of a picnic blanket under a tree, a garden table laid outside for tea, two deck chairs next to each other on a beach. It's the smell of a wooden porch warmed by the sun, the comforting unchangeability of a particular sitting stone or bench that marks a regular walk, the sight of a softly illuminated tent in contrast to the scale of a landscape around it.

When we sit in the sheltered wholeness of a garden enveloped and caressed by greenery and scent, light a lantern to shine into the night, take time to shower slowly, throw open our windows to let in fresh air or walk to work, we know hygge.

Hygge offers space for both reverie and relatedness. The heat of an open fire draws us close. Its shadow gives us a place to hide and softens our gaze. The naked togetherness and heat of a sauna, or

bathing alone outside in warm water, enveloped by dusk, green leaves and birdsong, both dissolves our boundaries and holds us in intimacy.

Hygge is our awareness of the scale of our existence in contrast to the immensity of life. It is our sense of intimacy and encounter with each other and with the creaturely world around us. It is the presence of nature calling us back to the present moment, calling us home.

Blessed are we who can laugh at ourselves for we shall never cease to be amused.

Proverb

Light-heartedness

The sense of aliveness and wellbeing that we know when we hygger is ultimately articulated by the eloquent presence of death. The contrast of darkness around us frames the illumination and warmth of a hyggelig moment and intensifies our pleasure.

In hygge there is an element of serenity in the recognition that we cannot quite grasp the mysterious character of the world, but choose to let go and simply let things be as they are. We relax and celebrate the moment, regardless.

Perhaps this particularly Danish focus on the ordinary and mundane, on 'hygge' and the creation of a space filled with familiar, comforting, ordinary things, cordons us off – albeit temporarily – from nothingness.

Christian Hall

Hygge is a devotion to making life enjoyable. It is lived in a spirit of lightheartedness and thrives on spontaneity. Hygge is more aligned to sensual pleasure and joy than deep reflection. Danes are always ready to laugh and to seize cause for celebration. They look for ways to invest any occasion with specialness.

A hyggelig occasion lifts our spirits and gives us a lightness of being, the atmosphere binding us together. It feels like a kind of enchantment, reminding us of what life is all about. We weave ourselves into the particulars of the place and feel at home with ourselves and with those around us.

In its aspect of comfort, hygge involves a sense of wellbeing which encourages relaxation and peacefulness. It excludes by definition a distracted or preoccupied state of mind: hygge is commitment par excellence to the present moment in its basicness. In the words of Hartmann-Petersen, 'Hygge rushes in of itself as soon as one is carefree.'

Judith Friedman Hansen

The Danish word *trivsel* means to thrive. When we hygger, we promote *trivsel* and wellbeing in ourselves and others, reclaiming some human dignity in a culture of relentless activity and productivity, and creating space for loving kindness. Hygge spreads wellbeing like the flame of a need fire out into the community.

5. Simplicity

He didn't remember,
he didn't worry, he just was.

Tove Jansson

Hygge is as simple as a candle, lit and placed on a windowsill to welcome someone home. It is both an inner and outer condition of simplicity; a clarity of presence and intention, and an honest, uncomplicated practice. In our over-stimulated lives with so much to distract our attention and pull us in opposing directions, we can turn to hygge as a conscious and appreciative approach to living. Hygge is a timeless practice, an everyday mindfulness that comes from a wholehearted participation in life.

There is a simple fidelity to the moment that we experience through hygge. We notice how a mug of morning coffee stands steaming on the table, how our bedside lamp and an old volume of poetry or a new lover beckon us to bed, how a familiar room slowly changes colour as morning arrives. When we hygger, we remove the clutter of perception and reach a singleness of purpose. By dimming the lights, putting the kettle on or laying out a picnic rug, we adjust our surroundings to guide our energy and desire. Hygge pays attention to the concerns of the human spirit, turning us towards a manner of living that prioritizes simple pleasure, friendship and connection above consumption.

Less is more.

Robert Browning

Simple pleasure

To spend an hour digging a flowerbed with a friend or to end a working day in a hot bath with the window open to the sound of evening folding in on itself on the street outside, are experiences infused with hygge. The familiarity of domestic routine and the delight inherent in simple pleasures evoke hygge – fresh bread,

an evening walk, pure wool, a kiss, a bike ride. Hygge is about having less, enjoying more; the pleasure of simply being. When we hygger, we experience abundance in contrast to the pervasive affluence in which many of us are starved of soulful experience. But hygge is not pinching and parsimonious. It is generous and celebratory, a way to remember the importance of the simple act of living itself.

I have no philosophy, my favourite thing is sitting in the studio.

Arne Jacobsen

Ordinariness

A single bloom on a kitchen table speaks of the simplicity that characterizes hygge – something modest, lovely and evanescent to show that we care.

Hygge is found in quiet generosity not grand gestures, in returning to the office with a coffee for a colleague or making breakfast in bed for our partner. There are minor and hidden things that contribute to a hyggeligt life that we notice only in their absence –

fresh bed linen, the box of candles that we reach for at the bottom of a cupboard, a photograph pinned to an office cubicle, the way that a flatmate routinely leaves a note and an extra portion of food for us in the fridge.

The aspects of things that are most important for us are hidden because of their simplicity and familiarity.

Ludwig Wittgenstein

It is in giving value to the ordinary things that we do, in seeing them as a significant part of the greater whole, that we learn to hygge. The challenges of our lives are far from simple. If we address everyday tasks in such a way that we take pleasure in doing them simply for their own sake, we move through our day as an annotation of moments, not a checklist. By listening to music while we sit in congested traffic, or enjoying the sensation of standing with our hands in a sink full of warm, soapy water, we make dignified – even joyful – work of essential tasks that we might ordinarily consider drudgery. It's easy to miss the windows of calm that open in our daily commute from one task and one place to the next.

Beauty in utility

Beauty and utility are at the heart of Scandinavian design. In Denmark, good design is part of national consciousness. Its cardinal virtues are practicality, simplicity and quality. The Danes value understatement and clean lines, a mixture of the relaxed and the precise. If something has purpose as well as beauty, it has integrity. Everyday objects are considered important, created to be durable and meaningful. Their outer simplicity contains a hidden plenitude. Calmness of form can encourage calmness of mood. The touch of handmade and well-crafted things evokes hygge. They speak to us of continuity, comfort, naturalness and care.

Have nothing in your house that you do not know to be useful, or believe to be beautiful.

William Morris

There is an enriching and integral nature that well-crafted things bring to our lives, and a power of enchantment that resides in a handcrafted object. When we use a simple, handmade item, there is an interplay that takes place between the object and our own emotions and state of mind. We encounter the possibility of simplicity in ourselves in what we hold in our hands. And we touch the life of the maker. There is a social and spiritual significance in bringing practical beauty into our homes, an invitation to live a life of real quality. But ultimately, quality of life is not tied to owning craft but to the careful crafting of our lives. Buying the perfect bread board doesn't lead to a life of simplicity. Slow living isn't the determined and nostalgic collecting of thrifted and lovely things to arrange and display. It is a mindful and intentional approach to living. Hygge helps us to slow down, to take time to find beauty in what seems ordinary.

Craft makes our homes more human.

Ilse Crawford

Authenticity

Simplicity is a way of being, not an acquired lifestyle. In recent years, many of us have slowly shifted our desire for labels and mass-produced goods towards the handcrafted and homemade. The pared down aesthetic that has been adopted by consumers around the world stems from values that Scandinavian cultures have quietly adhered to for years – the values of authenticity and simplicity that underpin hygge. But an aesthetic that appears to eschew ostentation can still be a marker of status in a different guise. Instead of visible consumption of brash and branded goods, the elegant trappings of a simple life can easily become cultural capital, symbols of taste and knowledge.

Although many Danes enjoy comfortable lives of material abundance, most resist display of status. In Denmark, hygge is considered antithetical to excess and held at a distance from excessive consumption. It is upheld of as a marker of authenticity, associated with an informal, intimate way of being and socializing that gives a sense of being distanced from status games. Hygge is thought to be lost when we indulge in luxury consumption or when we thirst to be noticed, no matter how simply we clothe that desire. Hygge isn't interested in our qualifications or appearance,

but in who we are and what we bring to the moment. Ideally, it draws us away from the brittle edges of our selves and pulls us towards a still, warm centre of simple presence, and connection.

Hygge is an atmosphere of unselfconscious wellbeing that disappears if an occasion is taut or manipulated. It cannot be bought or engineered, no matter how artfully we arrange a scene or orchestrate an occasion. If we approach hygge from its perimeters by attempting to craft and capture perfect moments, it will elude us. We can clothe ourselves and our homes in the accoutrements of a simple life but fail to reach the heart of the matter, that simplicity is a way of being not having. It affords us space and clarity to address the very real, and often messy, business of living and caring for one another. Hygge is not allied to the carefully pared-down and controlled but to generosity, paying attention and letting go. The pleasure is found in living hygge not curating it, in the experience of the journey not owning the map.

The effortless flow of conversation between two old friends, the worn surface of a kitchen table scratched with time and use, are hygge. The ease of interaction that comes from sincerity and authenticity, a desire to shelter not rise above each other. It is the raw authenticity of being unguarded and free.

Diversity

Real authenticity is found where we can feel human, in those places that emanate identity, relation and history. Hygge is revealed in the texture of the well-loved, worn and flawed. It's not attached to a particular aesthetic. It's not about style, but feeling and atmosphere. A home can be without conscious style but full of hygge.

It is how we relate to the things around us – the value that we give them through daily use – that is important. We can take as much pleasure in a neon-bright blanket or plastic ornament as in a wooden spoon. The accretions of a well-lived life, whether they can be contained in a single box in the back of a van, or in a family home overflowing with fridge magnets, post cards, sports kit and books, speak of hygge. Hygge is read in the story of a place and sung in tune with the lives that are lived there. But if our surroundings are too cluttered it is harder to make space to hygge. We can become haunted by the objects around us, by our entanglement in a web of meanings and past associations. Hygge requires clarity of presence that is difficult to achieve if we are burdened by things or at a loss to find what we need in a sea of possessions. If we keep only the things that are useful and that contribute to our sense of wellbeing, we naturally veer towards simplicity and a more hyggeligt life.

Hygge is a spirit of togetherness that is not attached to belongings but to honesty and warmth. The simplicity associated with hygge is clarity of intention and quality of attention and in the appreciation that nothing is perfect, nothing is finished, nothing lasts forever; that one moment will roll into the next and open us to another uncontrived opportunity for connection.

Material goods rarely alter our levels of happiness, unlike emotional experience. Having can never replace being.

Ilse Crawford

6. Observance

Hygge is a pervasive, all-year-round presence in Denmark that flourishes in any available space in life. Danes imbue most occasions – holidays, holy days and ordinary days – with the warmth and lightheartedness of hygge. Almost any moment is an opportunity to savour a feeling of belonging togetherness, from wedding celebrations to bedtime stories.

The observance inherent in hygge opens our eyes to the value of tradition and the quality of soul slightly concealed in the details and commonplaces of ordinary life – the objects that are most alive and connected to the world through daily use and the modest activities that we repeat.

Through hygge we mark special occasions and enjoy the elemental and ritual pleasures of everyday life. Sharing food, bathing, lighting a fire or walking home together can all be charged with meaning if done in the spirit of hygge.

Habit

Our habits shape us. We thrive on repetition. Like the lullabies of early babyhood, the predictable tempo of habit helps us fall into a place of ease and relaxation. The comforting structure of routine liberates our vitality and establishes a pleasurable and familiar pattern to our lives that stretches into the past and strengthens the present. At the heart of routine is the discipline that makes room for the remarkable in the mundane.

How we spend our days is, of course, how we spend our lives.

Annie Dillard

Hygge is so ordinary, so entwined with our daily lives that many of us don't realize that we already know how to do it. We all hygger naturally in the routine things that we do for comfort such as kicking our shoes off at the door, pulling down the blinds at night, running a bath at the end of a working day or putting on woollen socks first thing in the morning

before going downstairs to walk on the cold tiles of a kitchen floor. Everyday activities that appeal to our senses, like wrapping ourselves in a blanket or holding a mug of hot chocolate, and our actions that lead to a sense of connection, such as curling up together on the sofa to watch a film, making love, watering our plants or opening our front door to welcome a friend, all contribute to a hyggeligt life.

Hygge is there when we listen to the radio while we address emails, or share music as we wash the dishes together after an evening meal. It makes everyday tasks feel manageable and pleasurable. Tangles can be more easily teased from a child's hair with a candle lit on the edge of the bath and a story. An afternoon spent raking leaves together feels celebratory when it ends with an evening sitting beside a warm bonfire. Each one of us clears a path to hygge in our own way through the actions that we repeat, like dancers who take time to rehearse the same series of movements until they flow through them with grace and ease.

To affect the quality of the day, that is the highest of arts.

Henry David Thoreau

Attention

The practice of hygge keeps us alive to everyday enchantment. It is in the small gestures that we make when we pay attention to one another's needs like exchanging a houseguest's shoes for slippers or placing a cushion behind someone's back. And in the way we notice and address the things around us that ask for our attention – a squeaking hinge or a root-bound plant.

Hygge is hidden in our ephemeral daily experiences, such as watching how the light moves around our home, drawing us to different corners at different times of the day – to drink our first cup of tea on the porch or to read the paper in a last patch of sun at the end of the day.

We pay attention to the poetics of everyday life by celebrating a birth or deadheading roses at dusk. By bringing seasonal objects into our homes – dried seedpods, fresh flowers, pinecones or berries – we salute the changing seasons and celebrate the transitory that keep us alive to everyday enchantment.

Openness and empathy both characterize hygge. It is an attitude of respect and participation. By giving one another and ordinary activities our wholehearted attention, we begin to live more consciously, moment by moment.

Hygge is found in the contentment we feel when we really enter into what we are doing. It's often associated with hobbies, with the pleasure of being part of a sports team or working together on a creative project, like painting a mural or redecorating our homes. Through familiar pastimes like playing the piano, losing ourselves in the motion of a potters wheel, reading a novel or gardening, we enjoy hygge alone. With no one to consider but our selves it is easy to hygge and celebrate solitude.

The stillness at the heart of hygge helps us attune to wonder by facilitating pause, whether that is standing in front of a painting for a moment of unburdened contemplation or sitting back in our chair to revel in the closeness and love that emanates from a gathering of friends.

When we hygger, we relax and move deeply into a task or a moment so that its interiority stirs our hearts – cooking becomes time to savour the tastes and textures of the food we are preparing, a slow walk to work reveals the details of the streets we might ordinarily hurry along. Hygge is part of an intentional and appreciative approach to living that gently shifts our priorities and deepens our sense of what is extraordinary in ordinary life. It is rooted in the particular and branched towards the timeless. In the things

that we do to consciously celebrate our lives, we acknowledge both the present and the passage of time.

Attention is the rarest and purest form of generosity.

Simone Weil

Ritual

When we hygger, we ritualize the everyday things that we do and transform the commonplace. The smallest actions consciously and regularly repeated become the rites of everyday existence, shared or solitary, that speak to our hearts. Lighting a candle on waking eases us into the day. Allowing an extra ten minutes each morning for children to climb into our bed warms each one of us. Hygge is with us in our quiet kitchen when we boil the kettle, weigh out our coffee, choose a favourite mug and wait for it to brew. When we listen to a well-loved piece of music on the train or stop for morning coffee, when we read in a hammock at weekends or mark Friday afternoons in the office with cake and beer, we experience the hygge inherent in those moments as a touchstone at the centre of our busy lives.

In our deeds we can structure our lives so that the simple things that we do everyday, from bathing to cooking, have resonance and ritual.

Ilse Crawford

Bathing is often the only time that we have to feel wholly naked and alone. Lying in warm water and silence, we celebrate a private and ancient ritual. There is ritual and hygge in bedtime routines – calling dogs in from the garden and locking the doors, carrying a glass of water upstairs, drawing the curtains and brushing our teeth side by side; washing the day from our hands and faces, lighting a candle, turning on a bedside lamp, folding down the covers. Climbing into bed with a book or lying together with nothing to distract us, releases us into each other's arms and the embrace of sleep.

Through hygge, we create extraordinary moments in our ordinary lives strung like prayer beads that summon happy associations to reach for in difficult times. There are no intrinsically sacred objects or experiences; they are made sacred by the special context that we give

them. The way that we prepare a place to hygge is important. We create boundaries around an experience or a location to ensure that we feel comfortably held, whether that is by allocating time or defining literal parameters – setting aside an hour to enjoy tea with a neighbour, putting up a marquee or pulling chairs close around a table for dinner.

Keeping certain places protected and dedicated for special activities facilitates hygge – an armchair in a corner set aside for reading, a table left uncluttered to enjoy our hobbies. By creating a point of focus, we centre our selves and our environment. It only takes something as simple as a tea light on a coffee table or a carefully chosen film to invite hygge. Feeding our senses with warmth, good food, touch, fragrance or music adds to the ceremonial pleasure of hygge.

Cherished rituals feed our awareness and our desire to continue – even prolong – life. Hygge helps us to stay in touch with the rhythms of life, the cycles of our days and turning seasons. By paying attention to our natural patterns, we tap into the source of vitality that flows through the natural world around us.

The word rite, or ritual, comes from the latin word *ritus*, or river. Hygge is the pleasure of being immersed in the flow of life but allowing ourselves to eddy for a while. The moments after a wild swim when we stand wrapped in a warm towel, still feeling the kiss and pull of the water are saturated with hygge, with a feeling of connectedness and peace.

Other hyggelig rituals connect us to the flux and flow of life – tending a garden together, planting a window box, or visiting a city where the streets are lined with cherry blossom, an evening stroll along our neighbourhood street, a walk through the spicy, sweet water and rich earth scent of bluebells in spring, a cairn built on a hillside, added to over time by each person who walks the same path.

The Danish expression *at holde mørkning*, to hold twilight or watch it darken, describes the pleasure we take in pausing to observe as day slips into night. To stand at our window, wrapped in the half-dark and watch the day disappear behind the building opposite our own and the lights appear in the windows around us, is a moment of hygge.

Lighting a lantern on our doorstep at dusk marks the threshold between inside and outside, between day and night and helps us move from one sphere of experience into the next. When we dine by candlelight or walk under a full moon, we summon the solace of darkness.

We need communal ritual as well as private. When we eat in season, we celebrate our food and

179

the changing seasons more keenly. Picking the first strawberries of the year together after waiting all winter for them to appear or foraging for mushrooms in a seam of woodland tunes us into our local landscape. A visit to our nearest park or a stroll along a hedged lane to pick sloe berries after the first frost marks the shifting seasons.

Many cultures celebrate the equinox, particularly summer and winter when the difference between day and night are most clearly defined. Fire is a reoccurring symbol throughout the year in Denmark. At the time of the midsummer equinox, the shortest night of the year, Danes celebrate Sankt Hans Eve, the birthday of John the Baptist. The Christian festival is built upon the ancient pagan rituals of the summer solstice: the lighting of huge bonfires all over the country to acknowledge the full flourishing of the summer on a night full of northern light, magic and power when herbs were thought to be at their most potent. The old tradition of collecting and consuming magical herbs on that night has been replaced by gathering for dinner and drinks with family and friends. Then the fires are lit to banish all that is considered fearsome and dangerous, in the shape of witches and trolls, to a high mountain called Bloksbjerg. Along the miles of Danish coastline, the fires burn bright against the darkness

181

that seeps at the edge of the hygge, the fears and problems that we keep at bay.

Christmas in Denmark is the most hyggeligt time of the year. December is a month that glows with candlelight and the warmth of red hearts that decorate homes across the country. Many Danes also trim their houses with evergreen branches to bring life inside during one of the bleakest months of the year and represent the hope of renewal. On Christmas Eve, a fir tree is given pride of place and decorated with real candles. After feasting and drinking, electric lights are extinguished and the candles on the tree are lit. Everyone gathers around the tree, holding hands in a circle. Then they begin to sing, all moving in the same direction round and around the tree, dancing faster and faster until each person has enjoyed their chosen song, the gifts beneath the tree have been given out and the candles on the tree have burned low. This circle of figures united in spirit around a source of warmth and life, their backs turned away from the dark that surrounds them, must be the embodiment of hygge.

Celebration

Hygge is the red thread that runs through life in Denmark. Knotted into it are moments of celebration, ritual and quiet epiphany.

The spirit of festival is a small field that each one of us cultivates within ourselves, a place of freedom and spontaneity. It manifests throughout the year on the occasions that we chose to observe. In Denmark, the spirit of festivity is called *festlighed*. All parties, weddings, confirmations, graduations and birthdays are touched by this spirit and it enters into daily life and routine gatherings wherever people decide to invest a moment with specialness. Hygge and *festlighed* go hand in hand but the bigger the occasion the more diffused hygge becomes because it relies on intimacy and small-scale encounter.

Hygge is maintained with effort. Creating a space or an occasion to hygge takes time and care. But the preparations are part of the whole – chopping wood for a fire or putting up a tent, carrying rugs outside to sit under a tree, hanging fairy lights, buying fresh flowers or making decorations are all part of the pleasure of a hyggelig event.

For hygge to flow through a party, we need to prepare and meet in a spirit of generosity, in readiness to participate and celebrate the moment and each other. Hygge invites everyone to gather in an open mood, to contribute to an atmosphere of warmth and lightheartedness. The fabric of a party needs to be woven together by everyone present and a collective willingness to abandon ourselves to the rhythm of enjoyment without reservation, until the atmosphere envelopes us all. Each one of us makes an effort to make sure that an occasion is unforgettable, to capture the highlights, lace them into history and then elevate them to a treasured memory that we can return to and savour for years to come.

In Denmark, most festive occasions follow a similar pattern. Preparations are made well in advance – food is home-cooked, biscuits, bread and cakes are baked, parcels are carefully wrapped, flags are raised and a table thoughtfully laid and decorated with fresh flowers and candles. During the meal, there is singing from a treasure of national songs and many speeches are given – anyone can tap their glass and take an opportunity to say things that they might not express in everyday life.

When Danes raise their glasses in the air, look around the table into the eyes of each person present, say *skål* in unison and drink to one another, acknowledging the pleasure of the occasion, the atmosphere coalesces into a moment of pure hygge.

Observance writes the texts of our lives, creating stories to be shared in other hyggelige situations when we conjure the moment again. Traditions and rituals vary from one household and one culture to the next but the desire to celebrate life unites us all.

Through our thirst for connection, our future is created one gathering, one encounter, one moment at a time. Hygge rekindles our awareness of the importance and pleasure of mutuality and celebrates our interconnectedness. It keeps us engaged with the lifelong task of living in intimate and loving relation to the world around us.

We pass on the spirit of hygge through the quality of our presence. Ideas and values travel. Through hygge, each one of us can know a sense of deeper contentment that will radiate out from us into a global web of belonging togetherness.

Bibliography

Andersen, Benny, *Svantes Viser* (Borgen, 1972)

Andersen, Hans Christian, 'The Butterfly', *Complete Andersen's Fairy Tales* (Wordsworth Library Collection, 2009)

Bachelard, Gaston, *The Poetics of Space* (Beacon Press, 1969)

Campbell, John L., John A. Hall and Ove K. Pedersen, *The Danish Experience: National Identity and the Varieties of Capitalism* (McGill-Queen's University Press, 2006)

Crawford, Ilse, *A Frame for Life* (Rizzoli International Publications, 2014)

Crawford, Ilse, *Home is Where the Heart Is?* (Quadrille, 2005)

Dickinson, Emily, *Emily Dickinson's Letters* (Everyman Library, 2011)

Dillard, Annie, *The Writing Life*, (HarperPerennial, 1990)

Friedman Hansen, Judith, *We are a Little Land* (Arno Press, 1980)

Fromm, Eric, *Man for Himself: an Inquiry into the Psychology of Ethics* (Owl Books, 1990)

Fromm, Eric, *On Being Human* (Continuum International, 1997)

Fromm, Eric, *To Have or To Be?* (Harper & Row, 1976)

Jansson, Tove, *Art in Nature: and other stories* (Sort of Books, 2012)

Kierkegaard, Søren, *The Sickness Unto Death* (Penguin, 2008)

Levisen, Carsten, *Cultural Semantics and Social Cognition* (Walter de Gruytes & Co, 2012)

Linnet Trolle, Jeppe, 'Cozy Interiority' www.revues.org (2015) (De Gruyter Mouton, 2012)

Linnet Trolle, Jeppe, 'Money Can't Buy Me Hygge' Social Analysis Volume 55 Issue 2 (Berghahn Journals, 2011)

Moore, Thomas, *Care of the Soul* (Piatkus, 1992)

Moore, Thomas, *The Re-enchantment of Everyday Life* (HarperCollins, 1996)

Plath, Sylvia, *The Unabridged Journals of Sylvia Plath* (Anchor Books, 2002)

Sexson, Lynda, *Ordinarily Sacred* (University Press of Virginia,1982)

Thoreau, Henry David, *Walden* (Penguin Classics, 2016)

Wittgenstein, Ludwig, *Philosophical Investigations* (Wiley-Blackwell, 2009)

Contextual notes

Arne Jacobsen – twentieth-century architect and designer of iconic furniture and home wear, who defined Danish design identity; Christian Hall – Philiopher, chef and forager based in Århus, Denmark; Carsten Levisen – Linguist, cultural researcher and Professor at Roskilde University, Denmark; Jeppe Trolle Linnet – Danish anthropologist, leading authority on hygge, author and consumer culture expert, founder of Linnet Research; Josef Frank – Austrian architect who fled Nazism for Sweden. He worked for Svenskt Tenn and is considered to be one of Sweden's most influential designers; Ilse Crawford – London-based interior architect and home wear designer, academic and founder of Studioilse. Ilse created a range for iconic Danish brand Georg Jensen, has collaborated with Swedish brand Ikea and designed Ett Hem, a hotel in Stockholm; Knud Jespersen – Danish politician who was Chairman of the Communist Party of Denmark from 1958-77; Mogens Lorentzen – nineteenth-century Danish author, illustrator and artist best known for 'Christmas Tree with its Decorations'; Søren Kierkegaard – nineteenth-century Danish existentialist philosopher, poet, social critic and author; Tove Jansson – twentieth-century Finnish novelist and artist who created the beloved children's characters The Moomins.

Index

Acknowledgements

Thank you to my family for sustaining me with love and hygge during the weeks that it took me to write this book – my husband, Konrad, for his unflinching belief in me, our children Bella, Milo, Manu and Taya for their love and patience and my parents, Helle and Paul, for their insight, care and calm. My mother's Danish spirit is between the lines and in the margins of these pages.

Thank you to my sister, Birgitte, for sharing so many ideas, for her magnanimity and comfort, to my brother, Nicholas, for his reassurance and enthusiasm and to my aunts Hanne and Kirsten and my cousin Christian – their kindness, good humour and generosity have been an immeasurable support. And to my whole Danish family for teaching me the language of hygge.

I am indebted to Jeppe Trolle Linnet for his encouragement and for expanding the limits of my knowledge of hygge and to Judith Friedman Hansen for shaping my understanding. I must thank Ilse Crawford for her work from which I have drawn much inspiration. Many of the thoughts in this book are inspired by the writings of Thomas Moore and Lynda Sexson. Thank you to my friend, photographer Susan Bell for tenderly and patiently capturing my vision of hygge. And finally, I must thank Laura Higginson for asking me to write this book, Sally Somers for her thoughtful and meticulous edits and my friend and agent Sophie Hicks for her reassuring presence.

A final note

Hygge is dependent on having our most basic human needs met. Without security and shelter it's hard to survive. For every copy of this book bought a donation will be made by the author to a charity in support of the homeless.